PASCAL

PASCAL

Paul M. Chirlian
Professor
Department of Electrical Engineering
Stevens Institute of Technology

MATRIX PUBLISHERS, INC.
Beaverton, Oregon • U S A

To Barbara, Lisa and Peter

10 9 8 7 6 5 4

ISBN: 0-916460-28-2
Library of Congress catalog card number: 80-81872

Production: Patricia Miller
Illustrations: Scientific Illustrators
Printing: Pantagraph Printing
Editor: Merl K. Miller

Matrix Publishers, Inc.
11000 S.W. 11th Street
Beaverton, Oregon 97005

Preface

This is an introductory text on PASCAL. It is intended for students who have had essentially no experience with computer programming or computers. It can be used by college or junior college students, or by those who are interested in teaching PASCAL to themselves.

The various topics of PASCAL are presented in a simple manner so as not to confuse the beginner. This text discusses the running of programs both from a terminal and also via batch processing. The terminal should be connected either to a large computer or to a small microcomputer.

This book emplasizes the structured nature of PASCAL. Although the GOTO statement is discussed, virtually all the programs are GOTO-less. Topics such as top down programming are also discussed. Motivation for writing structured programs is given.

Not only is the PASCAL language discussed in detail, but ideas of debugging are also given. The writing of algorithms is also presented. The topic of documentation is stressed and the self-documenting nature of PASCAL is discussed.

The subject of PASCAL is discussed rather completely. Thus, when the beginner has gone through the text, he will be familiar with most of the aspects of PASCAL. It is hoped that the book will serve as a reference so that even advanced programmers can refer to it to refresh themselves on some details. To aid in this, several appendices indicate the salient points of PASCAL.

The book is organized so that a beginner can start running programs almost immediately. Many varied exercises are included at the end of each chapter. An instructor's manual containing solutions to typical exercises is available.

Acknowledgments

The author would like to express his gratitude to his colleagues Professors Alfred C. Gilmore, Jr. and Emil C. Neu for the many helpful discussions held with them during the writing of this book. He would also like to express his gratitude to his son Peter for his help with some of the programs.

Much loving gratitude and heartfelt thanks are again due my wife, Barbara, who not only provided me with constant encouragement but who also typed the rough and final drafts of the manuscript and copy edited the text.

Contents

1 Introduction to PASCAL Programming 1

Some Basic Ideas of Computer Operations 1
Basic Elements of PASCAL Programming Language 3
Some Simple PASCAL Programs 8
Running PASCAL Programs 15
Programming Errors—Basic Discussion 19

2 Fundamental Arithmetic Operations 23

Real Arithmetic 23
Integer Arithmetic 24
Heirarchy—Use of Parentheses 28
Mixed Mode Operations 30
Built In Mathematical Functions 31
Constants 35
The Syntax of Typical VAR Declarations 36

3 Input and Output 41

The READ and READLN Instructions 41
The WRITE and WRITELN Statements 45
The Format of Numerical Output 47
Printing of Text with Output 49

4 Control Statements—Basic Ideas of Structured Programming 55

Boolean Variables—Conditions 55
THe IF Statement 59
Unconditional Looping 65
Conditional Looping 67
Nested Loops 72
The Case Statement 73
Basic Ideas of Structured Programming 75
The GOTO Statement—The Label Declaration 80

5 Arrays 87

Singly Subscripted Arrays 87
The Type Declaration 92
Multidimensional Arrays 94
Assignment and Logical Expressions with Arrays 97

6 Characters and Strings 103

Character Variables 103
Operations with CHAR Variables 106
Strings of Characters 109
The Packed Array 116

7 Subprograms—Further Discussion of Structured Programming 121

The Procedure Subprogram 121
Use of Procedures with Arrays 127
The Function Subprogram 128
Recursive Use of Subprograms 130
Nested Subprograms 132
Forward References 134
Procedure and Function Parameters 136
Structured Programming—Modularization—Top Down Programming 137
Debugging Programs 139

8 Additional TYPE Specifications—Files 145

User Defined Types 145
Sequential Data Files 149
Strings and Files 154
Text Files 156
Input and Output—External Files 158

9 Sets . . . 161

Some Elementary Ideas of Set Theory . . . 161
PASCAL Set Manipulations . . . 163

10 The RECORD and Variant . . . 167

The RECORD . . . 167
THe WITH Statement . . . 170
Use of RECORD Arrays . . . 172
Nested RECORDs . . . 173
RECORD Variants . . . 177

11 Dynamic Data Structures . . . 183

Dynamic Data Storage . . . 184
Reusing Dynamic Storage . . . 190
Dynamic Data Structures . . . 193

Appendix A PASCAL Keywords . . . 199
Appendix B PASCAL Library Functions . . . 201
Appendix C PASCAL Structure TYPES . . . 203
Appendix D PASCAL Operators . . . 205
Index . . . 207

Chapter One

Introduction to PASCAL Programming

This book discusses the PASCAL programming language and how it can be used to write programs. We shall start with very basic ideas and then build up to more complex procedures.

The modern digital computer can do remarkable things. In a matter of seconds or minutes it can perform tasks that would take days or years to perform by hand. To the novice, computers may appear to "think," but they do not. The computer can only follow a detailed set of instructions called a *program*. In this book we shall discuss a language called PASCAL, which is used to program computers.

1-1. SOME BASIC IDEAS OF COMPUTER OPERATION

Before discussion programming, we shall briefly consider the makeup of a digital computer. This will help us to understand programming. The discussion of this section could apply to either a large digital computer which is housed in a computer center or to a small microcomputer which sits on your desk.

The main component of a computer is the *central processor* which performs all of the arithmetic and logical operations. For instance, it can add two numbers or compare them to see if they are equal. Also common to computers is the *main memory* which is used to store both the program that directs the computer and any data involved.

The main memory can supply data to the central processor at a very rapid rate, often in less than one microsecond (10^{-6} sec.) for each item. However, such memory is relatively expensive and its size is limited. It would be uneconomical to try to store extremely large quantities of data in main memory. For instance, if you have several computer programs which are run at different times, only the one program that you are presently using should be stored in the main memory. A similar situation applies with data storage. Suppose that a bank has 100,000 depositors. It would require too large a main memory to store all their account information in main memory. For these reasons, computers have additional memory which utilizes *magnetic storage*. For instance, data can be stored on magnetic tape such as that used by an ordinary tape recorder. Great quantities of data or many programs can be stored on tape. When you want to run one of these programs, the program is read from the tape and stored in the main memory. Both *hard* and *floppy disks* are also used for such storage. They function much more rapidly than tape storage. *Magnetic bubble* memories are also being used for these applications.

If a computer is to be useful, we must have a way of inputting programs and data and a way of outputting information. Some years ago, the primary means of supplying information to a computer was in the form of punched cards. Holes would be punched on cards using a *key punch*. The cards would then be read at high speed by a *card reader* which electrically sensed the positions of the holes. The output was printed out by a high speed line printer. Some large computer centers still function in this way. Programmers punch their programs and data on cards, and then take them to the computer center. The program is run at a later time and the results returned to the user. This is called *batch* processing, because the computer runs one batch at a time.

There is another form of input and output device called a *terminal*. The input is transmitted through a keyboard that resembles an ordinary typewriter keyboard. The programmer types in his program and the terminal generates electrical signals which supply the information to the computer. Output from the computer is typed on the terminal by the computer. This typing can be actually printed on a paper or it can appear on a video screen. The *video terminal* is, in general, faster and quieter than a printing terminal, but it does not produce a permanent copy. Often, video terminals have simple line printers nearby so that a printed or *hard copy* of the output can also be obtained.

Terminals are often used with large computers in a process called *timesharing*. Here, many programmers appear to use the computer simultaneously. Actually, the computer switches back and forth from user to user. However, the operation is often so rapid that each user thinks that the computer is his alone. While terminals are often used with small microcomputers, their operation is usually not in a time-sharing mode.

Digital computers can actually be instructed only by what is termed a *machine language program.* The commands are relatively simple, such as "store a number in a particular part of the memory" or "add a number stored in one memory location to a number stored in part of the central processor." It is extremely tedious to write programs in machine language. For instance, to perform simple multiplication requires many machine language instructions. To make the job easier for the programmer, special languages called *programming languages* are written. They are much easier for humans to use. For instance, suppose that we want to write a program that multiplies three numbers. That is, it corresponds to the algebraic equation

$$x = a \times b \times c \tag{1-1}$$

A statement written in the PASCAL programming language that corresponds to this one would be

$$\text{X:=A*B*C} \tag{1-2}$$

This closely resembles the algebraic equation and is easy for the human programmer to use.

A machine language program must actually direct the computer. For this reason, there is a program called a *compiler* that translates the programming language into machine language. However, the programmer who writes his program in PASCAL, or in any other programming language, is usually not concerned with the compiler. (Some programs are actually written in machine language, but in the great majority of cases, higher level languages such as PASCAL are used.) In the remainder of this book we shall discuss the writing and running of PASCAL programs.

1-2. BASIC ELEMENTS OF PASCAL PROGRAMMING LANGUAGE

In this section we shall discuss some of the basic elements of the PASCAL language. Like all languages, PASCAL is evolving so that the PASCAL whic is run on one computer installation may differ slightly from that run on another one. We shall attempt to point out these differences, whenever possible.

PASCAL Characters

In English, or in any other language, there are certain characters that can be used (e.g. the alphabet). Similarly, there are characters that are allowed in PASCAL. These include the 26 letters of the alphabet:

A B C D E F G H I J K L M N O P Q R S T U V W X Y Z

and the following symbols:

+ − * / := . , ; ? ' = <><=>>= ( ) [ ] { } : ↑ ..

Note that, on some computers, upper case letters are used while on others, lower case is used. These characters plus the blank space which we shall designate by "b" are used to write PASCAL programs.

Identifiers

In (1-2), a simple PASCAL statement, X, A, B, and C were all *identifiers*. That is, each was the name of some quantity. PASCAL allows the use of longer identifiers. This is usually helpful to the programmer since he does not have to remember what the identifiers designate. For instance, statement (1-2) might have been used to determine simple interest, that is,

$$\text{interest} = (\text{principal})(\text{rate})(\text{time}) \qquad (1\text{-}3a)$$

Statement (1-2) corresponds to this equation in that a quantity is calculated by multiplying three numbers. Another PASCAL statement that performs the same operation is

```
INTEREST:=PRINCIPAL*RATE*TIME                    (1-3b)
```

Statements (1-3b) and (1-2) are equivalent in that each directs the computer to perform the same operations. However, (1-3b) is superior in the sense that it serves to remind the human programmers of what calculation the program is directing, and of what quantities are used. The use of the longer name makes the program easier to read and the programmer is less likely to make mistakes.

The first symbol of an identifier should be a letter, but an identifier can include numbers as well as letters. For instance,

```
BOOK
NAME2
BOOKLIST
```

NA12BK3
HOUSE

are all valid identifiers. At times, other symbols such as $ may be allowed within an identifer, but this may not always be the case.

Identifiers should be eight characters or less in length. Actually, longer identifiers can be used as a help to the programmer. However, most implementations of PASCAL only look at the first 8 characters so that

LONGNAME

and

LONGNAME2

would be treated as the same identifier since only the first 8 characters would be considered. If you intend for LONGNAME and LONGNAME2 to represent different quantities, then an error will result. If you use long identifiers, make sure that identifiers which are to represent different quantities have at least one difference in their first 8 characters, or the computer will not distinguish between them.

Let us now give some examples of improper identifiers.

7BOOKS

is invalid because the first character is not a letter.

HOUSE,3

is improper because a symbol (the comma) is used. In general, if you start with a letter and use only letters or numbers, your identifier will be acceptable.

Remember that there may be many identifiers in long equations, so that you may find it helpful to use identifiers with more than 8 characters. Just be sure that the first 8 characters of two identifiers that represent different quantities are not identical.

Syntax Diagrams

At times, diagrams are used to represent the syntax, or structure, of PASCAL. Occasionally, instead of aiding our understanding, the diagrams may tend to confuse the beginner. Therefore we will always explain the syntax as well as draw the diagram. In Fig. 1-1 we illustrate the syntax diagram for the formulation of an identifier. The diagram is entered on the left side. The rectangular box indicates that the first character must be a letter. After leaving this box, you may loop around through the two remaining boxes or pass through to the output at the right hand side. This indicates that subsequent characters can be either numbers or letters. When there are alternative paths, taking any one of them will produce acceptable syntax. Thus, we have diagrammatically represented the previously discussed rules for identifiers.

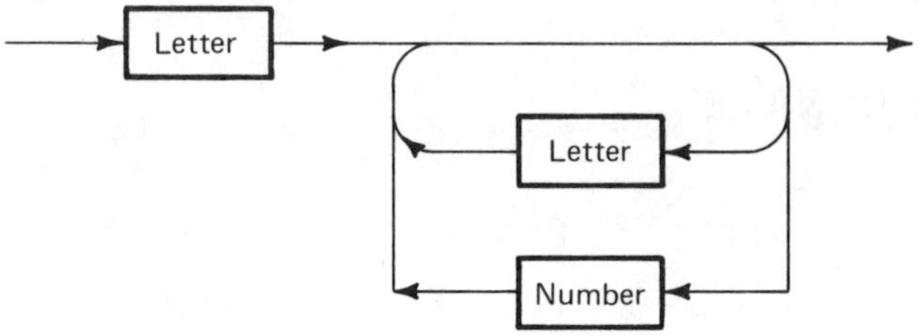

Figure 1-1. The syntax diagram for an indentifier

More complex syntax diagrams will include two types of symbols. In addition to the rectangular boxes of Fig. 1-1 which we have discussed, we can use a circle or a box with curved ends. The rectangular boxes actually refer to other syntax diagrams. For instance, in Fig. 1-1 there is reference to the syntax diagrams for letters and numbers. These are shown in Figs. 1-2a and b. Note that the symbols inside the circle or box with curved ends must be used *exactly* as written.

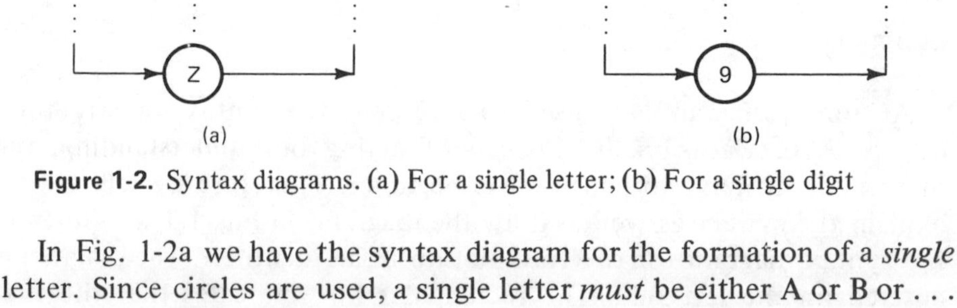

Figure 1-2. Syntax diagrams. (a) For a single letter; (b) For a single digit

In Fig. 1-2a we have the syntax diagram for the formation of a *single* letter. Since circles are used, a single letter *must* be either A or B or . . . or Z (one of the 26 letters of the alphabet). Note that there are no paths that allow looping back in this diagram. Hence, when it is followed, only a single letter results. In a similar way, Fig. 1-2b leads to the generation of a single digit.

Reserved Words-Keywords

There are certain words used in a PASCAL program that have special meanings. These are called *keywords* or *reserved words*. For instance, END. tells the compiler that the program is ended. Words such as this *cannot be used as identifiers*. The following is a list of reserved words.

AND
ARRAY
BEGIN
CASE
CONST
DIV
DO
DOWNTO
ELSE
END
FILE
FOR
FUNCTION
GOTO
IF
IN
LABEL
MOD
NILL
NOT
OF
OR
PACKED
PROCEDURE
PROGRAM
RECORD
REPEAT
SET
THEN
TO

```
TYPE
UNTIL
VAR
WHILE
WITH
```

Remember that no word on the list of reserved words may be used as an identifier.

PASCAL Program Structure

A PASCAL program is made up of identifiers, symbols, and keywords. Of course, they must be combined in a special way to form a program, just as the letters of the alphabet and the punctuation marks can be combined to form a story. This will be the topic of much of the remainder of the book. In the next section we shall consider writing a simple PASCAL program.

1-3. SOME SIMPLE PASCAL PROGRAMS

In this section we shall discuss some simple PASCAL programs. We start with a very simple program which adds 2.5 and 3.1 to obtain 5.6. The program is

```
PROGRAM ADD(INPUT,OUTPUT);                 (1-4a)
(*ADD TWO NUMBERS AND PRINT SUM*)          (1-4b)
VAR A,B,C: REAL;                           (1-4c)
BEGIN                                      (1-4d)
   A:=2.5;                                 (1-4e)
   B:=3.1;                                 (1-4f)
   C:=A+B;                                 (1-4g)
   WRITELN(C)                              (1-4h)
END.                                       (1-4i)
```

Let us consider this program. The first statement (1-4a) is the program title. It states that the program name is ADD. (Any valid identifier name could be used.) The (INPUT,OUTPUT) indicates that the program may use input and output devices. Note that this program will use only output devices so that INPUT is not needed. Actually, INPUT and OUTPUT are files through which the program communicates with the external environment. We shall discuss files in detail in Chapter 8.

For the time being, just write the INPUT and OUTPUT with a comma between them as shown in statement (1-4a). (Some PASCAL compilers do not require the (INPUT,OUTPUT). However, none will reject it.) The semicolon at the end of the line is a delimiter, and is used to separate one PASCAL statement from the next one.

The second line is called a *comment*. It is ignored by the compiler. It is merely included to explain the function of the program to the human programmer. Any material between (* *) will be treated as a comment and ignored when the program is compiled. Comments can be included throughout the program. Proper use of comments can help explain the program to human readers. We shall illustrate the use of comments throughout the text.

The third line declares all the identifiers used in the PASCAL program. In this simple program we have called the variables A, B, and C. The form of the line is the keyword VAR followed by a list of the variable names, separated by commas. There is no comma after the last variable in the list. Next there is a colon followed by the word REAL and the statement is terminated by a semicolon. Several things must be explained here. There are several types of variables that can be declared in a PASCAL program. We will discuss many of them in the next chapter, while others will be considered throughout the book. For the time being we shall restrict ourselves to REAL variables. A REAL number is an ordinary number with a fractional part and a decimal point, for example

```
 1.6372
 Ø.516
 2.167
-3.4682
```

Consider the second number in the list. A rule of PASCAL is that there *must* be a digit to the left of the decimal point. Hence, the Ø is required. That is, .516 would be rejected in a PASCAL program.

Note that the semicolon delimits (i.e. signifies the end of) the program statement, not the physical end of the line (that is caused by the line feed and carriage return). This is convenient. For instance, if we have a long list of variables, they need not all be physically on the same line. Therefore, statement (1-4c) could be written as

```
VAR A,
  B,C:REAL;                                    (1-5)
```

Note the indentation from the left margin. *It has no significance* to the

PASCAL compiler but its inclusion does make the program easier for the human programmer to read.

The actual steps of computation are between the words BEGIN and END. . Thus, the BEGIN starts the sequence of steps. The next line is

```
A:=2.5 ;
```
(1-6)

Let us consider this, When the program is compiled, the compiler scans the VAR line and reserves a location in the computer's main memory for each variable. Thus, in the program we are considering, three memory locations are reserved, one for A, another for B, and a third for C. Statement (1-4e) causes the value of 2.5 to be stored in the memory location for A. Similarly, statement (1-4f) causes the value 3.1 to be stored in the memory location for B.

Statement (1-4g) causes the values stored in the memory locations for A and B to be added and the result stored in the memory location for C.

Note that the symbol

```
:=
```
(1-7)

is not an equality. It causes a number to be stored in the memory location specified by the identifier on the left. If there is an expression to the right of the symbol, then it is evaluated and the result stored in the memory location to the left. After statement (1-4g) is executed, the desired answer is stored in the memory location called C.

The command

```
WRITELN(C)
```
(1-8)

causes the value stored in the memory location called C to be written on the output device of the computer. Hence, the result of running this program would be

5.6ØØØØ

Note that a fixed number of places will be printed. This number will vary from computer to computer.

The statement END. indicates to the compiler that the program is ended and compilation ceases. The final period (after END) is important. It indicates the actual end of the program. We shall subsequently discuss cases where END without a period is used.

Before proceeding, we must expand on some of the ideas that we have discussed. Let us start by considering the := sign. The general form of the statement which uses it is

```
IDENTIFIER:=Valid PASCAL operation;                    (1-9)
```

Note that there can only be a single identifier on the left hand side. Consider the following valid statement.

```
SUM:=ITEM1+ITEM2+ITEM3;                                (1-10)
```

Here, the numbers stored in the memory locations called ITEM1, ITEM2, and ITEM3 are added and the result stored in the memory location called SUM. The values stored in ITEM1, ITEM2, and ITEM3 are *not* changed by this operation. Only the value stored in the memory location of the identifier to the left of the := symbol is changed. Let us consider another valid statement.

```
SUM:=SUM+1.5;                                          (1-11)
```

This results in 1.5's being added to the value stored in the memory location called SUM. The result is then put back into SUM. Note that the old value of SUM is lost via this process. For instance, consider the sequence of statements

```
SUM:=2.0;                                              (1-12a)
A:=0.5;                                                (1-12b)
SUM:=SUM+A;                                            (1-12c)
```

After statement (1-12c) is executed, the value stored in SUM is 2.5. (Note the required zero before the decimal point in statement 1-12b.) The symbol := is called an *assignment*. For instance, in statement (1-12a), 2.0 is assigned to SUM.

Let us consider the use of semicolons in the program. Note that BEGIN does not require a semicolon after it. Actually, BEGIN and END determine a sequence of operations. We could in fact write program (1-4) in the following manner.

```
PROGRAM ADD(INPUT,OUTPUT);                             (1-13a)
(*ADD TWO NUMBERS AND PRINT SUM*)                      (1-13b)
VAR A,B,C:REAL;                                        (1-13c)
BEGIN                                                  (1-13d)
   A:=2.5;B:=3.1;C:=A+B;WRITELN(C)                     (1-13e)
END.                                                   (1-13f)
```

Note that a semicolon is *not* required after the end of line (1-13e) since WRITELN(C) is the last of the sequence of statements. In effect, BEGIN and END. serve as delimiters for this sequence. Actually we could also write the program as

```
PROGRAM ADD(INPUT,OUTPUT);                              (1-14a)
(*ADD TWO NUMBERS AND PRINT SUM*)                       (1-14b)
VAR A,B,C:REAL;                                         (1-14c)
BEGIN A:=2.5;B:=3.1;C:=A+B;WRITELN(C) END.              (1-14d)
```

Although this condensed form is perfectly good PASCAL, it is not desirable because it is hard for human programmers to read it and check for errors. In that respect, the form of the program shown in (1-4) is the best of those that we have considered. A syntax diagram illustrating the syntax of a sequence of operations, which is sometimes called a *compound* statement is shown in Fig. 1-3.

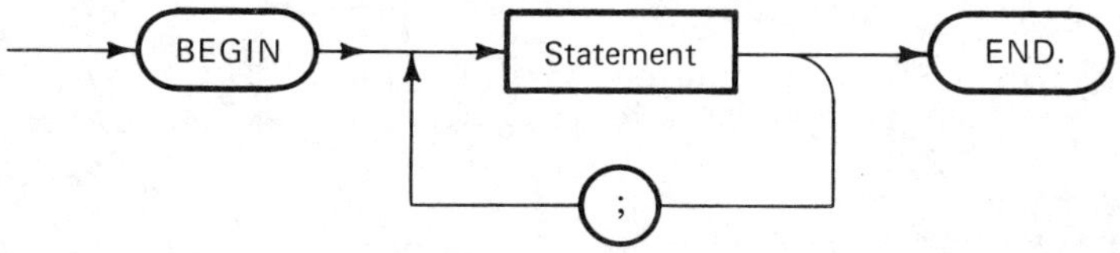

Figure 1-3. A syntax diagram for a compound statement. Note that we shall subsequently consider cases where the period is *not* required after the END.

If we had added semicolons after BEGIN and/or WRITELN(C), any of these programs would still have been good PASCAL. PASCAL allows a *null* statement, that is, a statement with nothing in it. For instance, if we put a semicolon after BEGIN, it is as though there were another statement (which was null) in the program between BEGIN and the semicolon in question. A similar statement could be made about a semicolon following WRITELN(C). Note that there *must* be a period after END since this indicates to the compiler that the program is over.

Another Program

The very simple program that we have considered only adds the numbers 2.5 and 3.1 to obtain 5.6. Let us keep the program simple but extend its versatility by allowing the person using the program to input any two numbers and have their sum computed. A program that accomplishes this is

```
PROGRAM ADDNEW(INPUT,OUTPUT);                           (1-15a)
(*INPUT TWO NUMBERS AND OBTAIN SUM*)                    (1-15b)
```

```
VAR SUM,INPUT1,INPUT2:REAL;                    (1-15c)
BEGIN                                          (1-15d)
   READLN(INPUT1);                             (1-15e)
   READLN(INPUT2);                             (1-15f)
   SUM:=INPUT1+INPUT2;                         (1-15g)
   WRITELN(SUM)                                (1-15h)
END.                                           (1-15h)
```

This program is similar to the previous one except for the two READLN statements. When the program is run, data is entered for the variables INPUT1 and INPUT2. For instance, suppose that you are running a program from a video terminal. When the program is run, the READLN statements require that data be entered. You would write a number on your video terminal and press RETURN. That number is then stored as INPUT1. Next, you would enter a second number and press RETURN. The second number is now stored in the memory location called INPUT2. There are variations of the READLN (and WRITELN) statement and we shall discuss them in a subsequent chapter. However, for the time being, we shall just use a very simple form, that is the statement

```
READLN(identifier);                            (1-16)
```

We shall discuss the entering of data in greater detail in the next section.

Printing of REAL Data

When REAL data is printed, it is usually in the form of a single digit followed by a decimal point and five significant figures. For instance, in program (1-15), if we entered data so that INPUT1 were given (assigned) the value 2.3 and INPUT were assigned the value 3.1, then the answer

5.4ØØØØ

would be printed. For numbers greater than 9.99999, the number would be printed using using *exponential notation*. That is, it is multiplied by a power of 1Ø. For instance, 26.3 would be represented as

2.63ØØØE1

where

E1 represents $1Ø^1 = 1Ø$

Similarly,

E2 represents $1\emptyset^2 = 1\emptyset\emptyset$

.

.

.

E6 represents $1\emptyset^6 = 1{,}\emptyset\emptyset\emptyset{,}\emptyset\emptyset\emptyset$
E−1 represents $1\emptyset^{-1} = \emptyset.1$
E−2 represents $1\emptyset^{-2} = \emptyset.\emptyset1$

Thus, $2.3 \times 1\emptyset^6$ would be represented as 2.3E6 while Ø.ØØØØ14326 would be represented as 1.4326ØE−5.

Note that exponential notation allows very large or very small numbers to be represented without using very many significant figures. With very many computers, the maximum value of the number following the E is 38. That is, we can use E38 and E−38, but E39 is too large for most computers to handle. This is termed an *overflow*. In such cases, computation would cease and all data is usually lost. In a similar way, if the number is smaller than Ø.1E−38, an *underflow* results and computation ceases. Note that some computers can work with exponents greater in magnitude than 38.

The E notation can also be used for data input. For instance, in response to the READLN statements of program (1-15) we could have responded with 1.23E6 and 1.342E7. The result in this case would have been 1.4651E7 (note that 1.23E6 = Ø.123E7). The number of significant figures need not be the same in each case.

Subtraction, Multiplication and Division

We have discussed programs that add real numbers. Now let us consider subtraction, multiplication and division. The PASCAL symbol for subtraction is the minus sign, for multiplication it is the asterisk (*), while the symbol for division is the slash (/).

As an illustration, let us write a program that computes a weighted average of five test grades. The formula that we shall use is

$$\text{ave} = \frac{\text{test1} + 2\text{test2} + 2\text{test3} + 2.5\text{test4} + 3.5\text{test5}}{11} \qquad (1\text{-}17)$$

A PASCAL program that performs this calculation is

```
PROGRAM WEIGHTEDAVE(INPUT,OUTPUT);
(*WEIGHTED AVERAGE OF 5 TESTS*)
VAR WEIGHTAVE,TEST1,TEST2,TEST3,
        TEST4,TEST5:REAL;
```

```
    BEGIN                                                  (1-18)
       READLN(TEST1);
       READLN(TEST2);
       READLN(TEST3);
       READLN(TEST4);
       READLN(TEST5);
       WEIGHTAVE:=(TEST1+2.Ø*TEST2+2.Ø*TEST3
                       +2.5*TEST4+3.5*TEST5)/11.Ø;
       WRITELN(WEIGHTAVE)
    END.
```

In this simple program, the computation is actually performed in the single line where WEIGHTAVE is obtained.

Note the use of the parentheses. They are used to group terms in PASCAL in much the same way that they are in ordinary mathematics. In the next chapter, we shall discuss mathematical operations in much more detail.

We have considered some simple PASCAL programs. In the next section, the procedures for running them will be discussed.

1-4. RUNNING PASCAL PROGRAMS

We shall now consider the running of PASCAL programs. Usually, as far as the programmer is concerned, one of two procedures is used. For instance, the program and any necessary data can be entered using punch cards and the program run using batch processing. Alternatively, the program can be entered on a (video) terminal, either in a timeshared mode on a large computer, or on a small computer controlled solely by the programmer. In either case, it appears as though the programmer is the only one using the computer. We shall discuss each of these procedures in turn. The reader need only refer to the actual mode of operation he is using.

Timeshared or Single-User Operation

In this mode of operation, the programmer types in the program essentially as though a typewriter were being used. When a timeshared computer is used, a log in procedure must be used. This varies from computer to computer, and the manual for your particular computer must be used to determine the appropriate procedures. Typically, when the terminal is connected to the computer (possibly over the telephone lines), the computer causes a message to be typed out, for instance

```
YOUR COMPUTER CENTER
PLEASE LOG IN
```
(1-19)

After the period, which is called a *prompt*, you would type in the appropriate information such as your user number and password. A typical log in procedure would cause the following to appear on your terminal:

```
YOUR COMPUTER CENTER
PLEASE LOG IN
.LOG
USER NUMBER
.1ØØ16
PASSWORD
.XWORD        (This will not show up on your terminal)
USER 1ØØ16 LOGGED IN
.PASCAL
PASCAL READY
```
(1-2Ø)

In this sample run, the text after the period is typed in by the user. After logging in, the PASCAL system is called up.

If the user is operating a small microcomputer, then the PASCAL system would usually be on floppy disks and when the system is "booted," these disks provide the programs that control the computer.

Let us assume that the timeshared or small computer is now "running" the PASCAL system. We will now discuss the procedures used to read, write and run a program. Usually, there is a program called an EDITOR that allows you to write text material, such as a program, and then change it if desired. Suppose that typing an E causes the EDITOR program to run. Then a sample run might be

```
.E
EDIT PROGRAM
FILE NAME
*SUBTRACT
MAKE PROGRAM SUBTRACT
PROGRAM SUBTRACT(INPUT,OUTPUT);
VAR X,A,B:REAL;
BEGIN
```
(1-21)

```
    READLN(A);
    READLN(B);          typed by user
    X:=A-B;
    WRITELN(X);
  END.
  (user types finish symbol)
  *
```

The first asterisk is a prompt given by the EDITOR. The EDITOR asks for the name of the program file. In this case, SUBTRACT has been typed. The EDITOR then instructs you to type in the program. After the program is finished, a symbol is typed that indicates to the EDITOR that the program is finished. The symbol will vary from computer to computer. It will be listed in your computer manual. The EDITOR then writes another * as a prompt. You can now instruct the EDITOR to save your program and then you can leave the EDITOR. Remember that the instructions that we have given here are only typical ones and that you should consult your computer manual for the specific ones. The manual will also list instructions that will allow you to change lines, and add or delete information.

After the program has been written, an instruction is given to the computer to compile it. If all is well, the program will compile properly and then an instruction can be given to run it. A message such as

```
PROGRAM SUBTRACT RUNNING
```

will be printed on your terminal. Now, in response to the READLN statement, the data must be entered. Each item of data must be entered on a separate line. (We shall consider additional procedures for entering data in a subsequent chapter.) In the simple case, after the second item of data is entered, and the RETURN pressed, the computation will proceed and the result will be printed on the terminal.

Batch Processing

When the program is to be run in a batch processing mode, all information is punched on a "deck" of punched cards. The cards are produced on a device called a *keypunch*. It is operated from a keyboard that is similar to a typewriter or terminal. However, now each line of text is punched on a separate card. For instance, each line of a PASCAL program is punched on a new card, and the data is also punched on cards.

Several other cards must be added to the program. These indicate who the programmer is, what his password is, when execution of the program should begin, and when the program has ended. For instance, a deck of cards to be used for a simple subtraction program could look like (remember that each line represents a single card):

```
JOBCARD
PROGRAM SUBTRACT(INPUT,OUTPUT);
VAR X,A,B:REAL;
BEGIN                                    (1-22)
   READLN(A);
   READLN(B);
   X:=A-B;
   WRITELN(X)
END.
JOBEXECUTE
1.63E2
2.48E2
JOBEND
```

The JOBCARD supplies the program name, password, etc. The program then follows. Each line corresponds to a separate card. The JOBEXECUTE card results in the program's being compiled and then run. Any data is punched on cards which follow this one. Thus, the data for the two READLN statements is supplied on the next two cards. There should be a separate data card for each READLN statement. The data cards are read in order. The first READLN statement assigns the value given in the first data card, etc. We shall discuss more versatile procedures for entering data in Chapter 3. After the program is entered, the computer will print

4.11ØØØE1

as the result of the computation. The JOBEND card signifies that all the cards have been read and that the computer is "finished" with the deck.

Note that the information punched on the various JOB cards will vary greatly from one computer center to another. Your computer manual should be consulted to determine the appropriate information.

In this section we have assumed that the program that you wrote was correct. In practice, most programs have errors in them. We shall discuss this briefly in the next section and in detail in a subsequent chapter.

1-5. PROGRAMMING ERRORS—BASIC DISCUSSION

Almost all programs contain some errors. This may be discouraging to the beginning programmer, but it should not be so. Experienced programmers know that removing errors, or *bugs* as they are called, is a part of programming. In a subsequent chapter we shall discuss *debugging* in detail. In this section we shall just mention some typical bugs that can occur and suggest some simple procedures for eliminating them.

The simplest type of error is a mistake in syntax. That is, you have not followed the rules of PASCAL. For instance, a required semicolon at the end of a line may have been omitted or you may have forgotten to declare a variable in the declaration statement. Such errors will be detected at compilation time. In fact, the program will *not* compile. Instead, a set of error messages will be printed and the "incorrect" statement will be printed out.

At times, such error diagnostics can be misleading. For instance, suppose that you have forgotten to declare a variable. The compiler may not indicate an error in the VAR statement but, instead, may point to an error in the first statement in which the undeclared variable is used. Of course, this statement is correct. It is actually the VAR statement that is in error.

Confusing error messages can also result if a BEGIN statement is omitted. The error message again may point to a different statement which is, itself, correct. Experience will make the error messages more meaningful. Of course, there are many occasions where the error message does indicate the incorrect statement. Most syntax errors can be corrected by a careful rereading of the program.

Another type of error is the *logical* error. In this case, the program may be perfectly good PASCAL, but still not calculate what you intended it to. For instance, suppose that in program (1-18), you inadvertantly typed a minus sign in place of one of the plus signs. The program would run properly but a *wrong answer would be obtained.* Whenever you write a program, no matter how simple, you should *always* check your result. For instance, check the answer using a hand calculator, with *several different* sets of data, so that you know that the program is functioning properly. This point cannot be emphasized too strongly. *Always check your program!*

Debugging of logical errors can be accomplished in a number of ways which shall be discussed in Sec. 7-9 after we have studied more

PASCAL. For the time begin, read through your program. This often catches typographical errors. Also go through your program step by step just as the computer does. This often shows up logical errors. That is, you may find that you are not calculating what you thought you were. We shall see that the structure of PASCAL is such that programs can be written that are either easily debugged, or which have few errors to begin with.

When you discover an error, then your program must be changed. If it is punched on a deck of cards, then the card (or cards) which has errors can be replaced by the programmer. If the program is being run from a terminal, then the EDITOR is used. There are various types of EDITORS. In the simplest, a line with an error must be retyped, just as a card is replaced in batch processing. The better EDITORS have procedures whereby characters can be changed in a line. Characters can also be inserted or deleted. There are search procedures wherein a desired character or group of characters can be found anywhere in the program and replaced. The manual for your EDITOR will tell you its capabilities and how to use it.

EXERCISES

1. Describe the functions of the components of a computer.
2. What is the function of a compiler?
3. List the allowable characters used in PASCAL.
4. List 5 valid PASCAL identifiers.
5. Comment on the use of these two identifiers.

   BOOKPAGENUMB6
   BOOKPAGENUMB7
6. Describe the form of PASCAL syntax diagrams.
7. List the PASCAL reserved words.
8. Discuss the use of comments in PASCAL programs.
9. Write a PASCAL program that evaluates

$$x = \frac{(a+b)(a-b)}{2c}$$

Run this program on your computer using the values

a = 2.3E3
b = 4.1E2
c = 2.41E–3

1∅. Repeat Exercise 9 for

$$x = (a+b)/(a-b)^2$$

11. Write a PASCAL program that evaluates the two functions

$$y = \frac{(a+b)(c+d)}{a-3(a+b)} \qquad x = \frac{(y+a)(y+b)}{2y}$$

Run the program on your computer using the values

a = 2.327
b = 34.26
c = ∅.1∅∅1E3

12. Repeat Exercise 11 but now, for the value of x, calculate

$$x + \frac{(y+a)(y+b)}{2y}$$

where the initial value of x is 1.23E2.

13. Repeat Exercise 11 but now use

$$y = \frac{(a^2+b^2)(a-b)^2}{(c^3+d)^2}$$

14. Write a PASCAL program that calculates factorial n (i.e. n!) for n = 6, that is

6(5)(4)(3)(2)(1)

Chapter Two

Fundamental Arithmetic Operations

This chapter shall cover the various types of arithmetic operations that can be performed in PASCAL. We begin with a discussion of arithmetic operations. In the last chapter, REAL arithmetic was introduced. The discussion will now be extended and other kinds of variables shall be considered.

2-1. REAL ARITHMETIC

The REAL numbers are the usual numbers with decimal points that were discussed in the last chapter. It is assumed that the reader is familiar with this discussion. For completeness, we shall briefly review. All REAL variables are declared using the keyword REAL. Such variables are said to be of type REAL. For instance,

```
VAR A,BOX,AVERAGE:REAL;
```
(2-1)

The PASCAL symbols for arithmetic operations are

addition	+	
subtraction	–	(2-2)
multiplication	*	
division	/	

Let us write a simple PASCAL program that implements the following arithmetic expressions.

$$x = a^2 - \frac{b^2 c^2}{a} + 2c \qquad (2\text{-}3a)$$

$$y = x + a^3 - \frac{b^2}{2} \qquad (2\text{-}3b)$$

and then prints out the values of x and y. The program is

```
PROGRAM SIMPLEMATH(INPUT,OUTPUT);
(*TWO ALGEBRAIC EXPRESSIONS ARE EVALUATED*)
VAR A,B,C,X,Y:REAL;
BEGIN                                                    (2-4)
   READLN(A);
   READLN(B);
   READLN(C);
   X:=A*A-B*B*C*C/A+2.Ø*C;
   Y:=X+A*A*A-B*B/2.Ø;
   WRITELN(X);
   WRITELN(Y);
END.
```

The program follows the ideas discussed in Chapter 1. The actual computation is directed in statements 8 and 9 where X and Y are calculated. In subsequent sections of this chapter we shall discuss additional arithmetic operations and then consider some more complicated programs.

2-2. INTEGER ARITHMETIC

PASCAL, as well as most other programming languages, makes a distinction between real numbers and integers. An integer is a number that has no fractional part, such as

1
1234
−1637

In PASCAL, it would be wrong to put a decimal point or an E in an integer. The reason that the distinction is made between real and integer quantities is that, in a computer, arithmetic with integers is simpler and can be performed more rapidly than the corresponding arithmetic with real numbers. Also, as we shall discuss, integer arithmetic is exact, while real arithmetic is only approximate. Of course, when we deal with real numbers, as we usually do in computation, we must use REAL variables.

Integers are declared using the expression INTEGER. For instance,

```
VAR ABLE,BOOK,K,BOX:INTEGER;                             (2-5)
```

declares that the variables ABLE, BOOK, K and BOX are integer variables. They are said to be of type INTEGER.

There can only be *one* VAR declaration in a PASCAL program. (We shall modify this statement subsequently when we consider subprograms.) The single VAR statement is used to declare all of the variables. For instance,

```
VAR LIST1,ITEM,ABLE:INTEGER;                    (2-6)
    KEE,TOM,X,Y:REAL;
```

declares that LIST1, ITEM and ABLE are INTEGER variables, while KEE, TOM, X and Y are REAL variables. Note that the word VAR is only written once, and that there are semicolons after INTEGER and REAL. The indentation of the second line is not necessary but it makes the statement easier to read.

Addition, subtraction and multiplication of INTEGER numbers are performed in the same way as they were for REAL numbers. For instance, suppose that we want to perform the following algebraic operation with integers.

$$x = a + bc - d$$

The following segment of a PASCAL program accomplishes this.

```
.
.
.
VAR X,A,B,C,D:INTEGER;                          (2-7)
.
.
.
X:=A+B*C-D;
```

When integers are divided, the procedure is different from that for reals. The symbol for integer division is

```
DIV
```

For instance, to write $x = a/b$, we use

```
VAR X,A,B:INTEGER;
  .
  .
  .
X:=A DIV B;                                     (2-8)
  .
  .
  .
```

The result of an integer division is an integer. This can lead to some unexpected results. For instance, suppose that in the above example, prior to the division, A had been assigned the value 8 and B the value 2, i.e.

```
A:=8;
B:=2;
```

Then the result would be 4 as expected. However, suppose that we assigned

```
A:=9;
B:=2;
```

The result would still be 4. Let us explain this. The result of an integer division is itself an integer. Thus it cannot contain a fractional (decimal) part. This part will be disregarded. Hence, if we take 9/2 = 4.5, the Ø.5 is disregarded and the result is 2. In general, the result of integer division is the closest integer that is *less than or equal* to the actual result. For instance, if A:=2Ø and B:=7;, then A DIV B results in 2 (i.e. 2Ø/7 = 2.8571).

Care must be taken when the result of an INTEGER division is negative. Remember that −3 is smaller than −2 which, in turn, is smaller than −1. Hence, if we have A:=−2Ø; and B:=7;, then A DIV B results in −3. Similarly, if A:=−5; and B:=2; , then A DIV B results in −3.

The remainder in integer division is not really lost. There is another operation that can be used to retrieve it. It is called

MOD

For instance, if A:=25; and B:=7;, then

A DIV B results in 3 (25/7 = 3 + $\frac{4}{7}$)

and

A MOD B results in 4

Let us consider another example. If A:=2Ø; and B:=7;, then

A MOD B results in 6 (2Ø/7 = 2 + $\frac{6}{+}$

A MOD B results in 6 (2Ø/7 = 2 + $\frac{6}{7}$)

Now let us consider negative numbers. Suppose that we have A:=−2Ø; and B:=7;. Then

$$-2\emptyset/7 = -3 + \frac{1}{7}$$

Remember the rules for division of negative integers. Now,

A MOD B results in 1

Next, let us consider the case where A:=2Ø; and B:=−7;.

$$2\emptyset/-7 = -3 + \frac{-1}{-7}$$

The remainder in this case is −1. Thus, we have

A MOD B resulting in −1.

Note that −2Ø/7 and 2Ø/(−7) produce different results when the MOD operation is applied. Hence, care should be taken when this operation is used.

Accuracy of REAL and INTEGER Operations

There are differences between REAL and INTEGER calculations. For instance, consider the real operation of 1.Ø/3.Ø. The result is Ø.333333333... . The computer can only work with a finite number of significant figures. Then, when 1.Ø/3.Ø is performed, there will be a slight inaccuracy. Since the number of significant figures is limited, there may also be inaccuracies in addition, subtraction and multiplication. The error due to loss of significant figures is called a *roundoff error*. Generally, so many calculations are performed in computer programs that the roundoff errors can accumulate, causing a relatively large error to result.

When INTEGERS are manipulated, the results are exact and no roundoff occurs. However, there are circumstances when REAL numbers must be used. Most arithmetic calculations must be performed with REAL numbers because the accuracy of the computation depends on fractional parts. The maximum allowable size of integers is much smaller than that of REAL numbers. For instance, on some computers, the allowable INTEGER range is between −32768 and 32767. On other computers, the range may be larger. Your computer's manual should be checked to determine the allowable range. If you exceed the allowable range of integers, some computers will cease operation. However, others may produce erroneous results. Thus, care must be taken when INTEGERS are used. Remember that most mathematical calculations involve the use of REAL numbers.

2-3. HIERARCHY—USE OF PARENTHESES

When an algebraic expression is evaluated, the operations are performed in a certain order. For instance, suppose that we have the equation

$$x = ab + c/d \tag{2-9}$$

We know that this means to multiply a by b, then divide c by d, and finally take the sum of the results. That is, Eq. (2-9) can be written as

$$x = (ab) + (c/d) \tag{2-10}$$

Here, the parentheses clarify the result, but they are not necessary. However, suppose that we want to add ab to c and *then* divide the result by d. Now we must use parentheses and write

$$x = (ab+c)/d \tag{2-11}$$

The order in which operations are performed is called a *hierarchy*. We have seen that the hierarchy can be modified by the use of parentheses.

Before considering the hierarchy of PASCAL, let us consider one more operation, that of *negation*. Suppose that we want to replace a variable with its negative. This can be accomplished by placing a minus sign before the variable. For instance,

```
B:=-A;                                    (2-12)
```

will result in the negative of A's being stored in memory location B. Note that two mathematical operational signs cannot be placed next to each other. For instance,

```
BOX:=ITEM*-NUMBER;
```

is *incorrect*. However, parentheses can be used to separate the two adjacent signs. For instance, the following is a valid statement

```
BOX:=ITEM*(-NUMBER);                      (2-13)
```

Now let us consider the rules of hierarchy in PASCAL. The PASCAL expression is scanned from left to right and the operations are performed in the following order:

First: negation
Next: multiplication (*) or division (/, DIV, or MOD)
Finally: addition (+) or subtraction (−)

For instance,

```
ANSWER:=ITEM+ABLE*SUM;                    (2-14a)
```

is equivalent to

```
ANSWER:=ITEM+(ABLE*SUM);                          (2-14b)
```

In a similar manner,

```
RESULT:=FIRSTSUM+SECONDSUM
                         DIV NUMBER;              (2-15a)
```

is equivalent to

```
RESULT:=FIRSTSUM+(SECONDSUM
                         DIV NUMBER);             (2-15b)
```

Parentheses

Just as in ordinary algebra, parentheses can be used to obtain more versatility. For instance, suppose that we want to evaluate

$$x = \frac{a-b}{c+d} \tag{2-16a}$$

A PASCAL statement that accomplishes this is

```
X:=(A-B)/(C+D);                                   (2-16b)
```

The PASCAL rules for parentheses are similar to those for algebra. First, *each* expression within a pair of parentheses is treated as a separate expression. These subexpressions are evaluated using the rules of hierarchy. Now each evaluated pair of parentheses is treated as a separate quantity. The resulting statement is then evaluated using the rules of hierarchy. Let us consider one additional example.

```
X:=(A+B)*(C+D)/(A-B)+C;                           (2-17a)
```

is equivalent to the algebraic expression

$$x = \frac{(a+b)(c+d)}{a-b} + c \tag{2-17b}$$

Note the asterisk in expression (2-17a). It is required. In PASCAL we cannot have (A+B)C+D), and *the multiplication sign must be used.*

Let us consider a more complicated algebraic expression

$$x = [(a+b)(c+b)+d](a-b) \tag{2-18a}$$

We have used both brackets and parentheses here. In PASCAL we can only use parentheses for this purpose. However, pairs of parentheses can be nested within other pairs of parentheses. Thus, a PASCAL expression that is equivalent to (2-18a) is

```
X:=((A+B)*(C+B)+D)*(A−B);                                  (2-18b)
```

These are called *nested* parentheses. The rule used is that the expressions within the inner pairs of parentheses are evaluated first. Each evaluated expression is then treated as a single variable. Then the evaluation proceeds starting with the expressions within the outer pairs of parentheses. We have illustrated two orders of nesting but there can be more, and the preceding rules still apply. That is, evaluation starts with the innermost pairs of parentheses and then proceeds outward. A very common syntax error is to omit one of the parentheses. The programmer should always check to see that the number of left parentheses equals the number of right parentheses.

2-4. MIXED MODE OPERATION

Thus far, we have written PASCAL statements which consisted solely of REAL or solely of INTEGER variables. Under certain circumstances it is possible to have both REAL and INTEGER variables in the same expression. This is called *mixed mode operation.*

Some types of mixed mode operation are acceptable while others are not, and will not compute. In general, an INTEGER quantity can be assigned to a REAL variable. However, the converse cannot be done. For instance, the following is acceptable.

```
PROGRAM MIXEDMODE(INPUT,OUTPUT);                (2-19a)
VAR REAL1,REA,ABLE,BOX:REAL;                    (2-19b)
     ITEM,W,X:INTEGER;                          (2-19c)
BEGIN                                           (2-19d)
  ITEM:=5;                                      (2-19e)
  W:=2;                                         (2-19f)
  X:=4;                                         (2-19g)
  REAL1:=6.3;                                   (2-19h)
  ABLE:=REAL1+ITEM/W;                           (2-19i)
  BOX:=ITEM MOD X;                              (2-19j)
  REA:=REAL1+ITEM DIV W;                        (2-19k)
  .
  .
  .
END.
```

Consider statement (2-19i). The slash indicates a REAL division. Hence, ITEM/W (5/2) results in 2.5. That is, the INTEGER variables are treated as though they were REAL. Hence, the value assigned to REAL1 is 8.8 (6.3+2.5). That is, in the division, ITEM and W are treated as REAL because of the REAL division. On the other hand, in (2-19k), an INTEGER division is performed. ITEM DIV W results in 2 (this is an INTEGER operation). Hence, the value assigned to REA is 8.3 (6.3+2). Similarly, as a result of (2-19j), the value assigned to BOX is 1.

If an INTEGER variable is on the left hand side of the assignment sign then, in general, a REAL variable cannot be on the right side of the assignment sign. For instance, the following would not be allowed in program (2-19)

```
ITEM:=W/X;            (2-20a)
X:=ABLE;              (2-20b)
W:=REAL1+ITEM;        (2-20c)
```

All are unacceptable because they attempt to assign REAL values to INTEGER variables. In the next section we shall discuss a procedure whereby the INTEGER part of a REAL variable can be assigned to an INTEGER variable.

2-5. BUILT IN MATHEMATICAL FUNCTIONS

In addition to the arithmetic operations of addition, subtraction, multiplication and division, PASCAL supplies additional mathematical functions. These are called *built in* or *library* functions. Let us consider some of these. For instance,

```
SQRT(identifier);     (2-21)
```

is used to take the square root of the listed identifier. For example,

```
.
.
.
VAR NUMBER,RT:REAL;
.
.
.                     (2-22)
NUMBER:=4.Ø;
RT:=SQRT(NUMBER);
.
.
.
```

The value stored in the memory location called RT will be $\sqrt{4}$ =

2.ØØØØØ. Similarly, if NUMBER were assigned the value 2.Ø, then RT would be assigned the value 1.41421.

In program segment (2-22) NUMBER is called the *argument* of the SQRT function. The argument of the SQRT function *must* be either positive or zero. The argument can be either REAL or INTEGER, but the result must always be REAL. It is said that SQRT *returns* a REAL answer. For instance, if we have

```
ANS:=SQRT(ARGUMENT);                                   (2-23)
```

then ARGUMENT can be either REAL or INTEGER, but ANS must be REAL.

The argument of a function need not be a simple variable. It may also be an expression. For instance,

```
ANS:=SQRT(X+Y*Z);                                      (2-24)
```

Let us consider some other mathematical functions.

LN(X) returns the natural logarithm of x

EXP(X) returns e^x

X may be REAL or INTEGER, but the result must always be REAL. The argument of the LN function *must* be positive.

As an illustration of the use of these functions, let us write a PASCAL program that raises a number to the ⅓ power. When complex programs are written, an *algorithm*, or procedure that performs the desired operation, must be obtained. Actually, the programming language is just a detail in obtaining a program. The "intellectual" part of the program is obtaining the algorithm.

In this case we shall use the following mathematical operations. If x is the number that we want to raise to the ⅓ power, and y is the result, then we can use the following equation.

$$y = e^{1/3 \ln(x)} \tag{2-25a}$$

Note that

$$e^{ab} = [e^b]^a \tag{2-25b}$$

and

$$e^{\ln(c)} = c \tag{2-25c}$$

The program is

```
PROGRAM FRACTIONALPOWER(INPUT,OUTPUT);                 (2-26a)
VAR X,Y,Z:REAL;                                        (2-26b)
```

```
BEGIN                                      (2-26c)
   READLN(X);                              (2-26d)
   Z:=LN(X);                               (2-26e)
   Z:=Z/3;                                 (2-26f)
   Y:=EXP(Z);                              (2-26g)
   WRITELN(Y)                              (2-26h)
END.                                       (2-26i)
```

The actual computations are performed in statements (2-26e), (2-26f) and (2-26g).

This program can be used to raise a number to any power. If statement (2-26f) were replaced by

```
Z:=A*Z;                                    (2-27)
```

then the program would compute the value of x^a.

Some other PASCAL functions are those which give the sine, cosine and arctangent. They are

```
SIN(X)                                     (2-28)
COS(X)                                     (2-29)
ARCTAN(X)                                  (2-3Ø)
```

In each case, the argument may be REAL or INTEGER but the result is always REAL. The argument of SIN or COS is expressed in radians (not degrees). Similarly, ARCTAN returns an answer in radians.

Let us consider another function,

```
ABS(X)                                     (2-31)
```

which returns the absolute value of X. For instance, if X:=–26.3, then ABS(X) returns 26.3. If X:=26.3, then ABS(X) returns 26.3. That is, ABS returns the magnitude of the function. If X is REAL, then ABS(X) is REAL. If X is INTEGER, then ABS(X) will be INTEGER. This is in contrast to the other functions that we have considered. Another function of this type is

```
SQR(X)                                     (2-32)
```

This returns the square of X (i.e., x^2).

There are two functions that are used to convert REAL values to INTEGER values. One is

```
ROUND(X)                                   (2-33)
```

Here, X is REAL and the result is an INTEGER, equal to the rounded value of X. For instance, if X:=26.4, then ROUND(X) returns the

INTEGER 26. On the other hand, if X:=26.5; or X:=26.6;, then ROUND(X) returns INTEGER 27. Similarly, if X:=−26.6;, then ROUND(X) returns −27.

A similar function is TRUNC(X). This truncates (throws away) the fractional part of a REAL number, so that if X:=26.3;, or X:=26.999;, TRUNC(X) returns 26. For negative numbers, the result is the same. If X:=−26.9; or X:=−26.7; or X:=−26.ØØ1, then TRUNC(X) returns −26. That is, TRUNC drops the fractional part. These functions convert REAL variables to INTEGER variables. In the last section we discussed procedures for converting INTEGER variables to REAL variables.

There are two functions that require INTEGER arguments and return INETGER results. They are

```
PRED(X)
```
(2-34)

and

```
SUCC(X)
```
(2-35)

PRED returns the predecessor value of the argument. For instance, if X:=3;, then PRED(X) returns 2 and if X:=−3;, then PRED(X) returns −4. Similarly, SUCC returns the successor value of the argument. For instance, if X:=3;, then SUCC(X) returns 4 and if X:=−3, then SUCC(X) returns −2. These functions appear to be trivially simple. However, in Chapters 6 and 8 we shall consider some practical uses for them.

In the functions that we have discussed, the arguments have been represented as X. Actually, the argument could be a simple arithmetic expression. We have listed some commonly used functions in this section. In the appendix we shall indicate a more complete list.

As an example of how built in functions are used, let us compute the roots of the quadratic equation

$$ax^2 + bx + c = \emptyset \tag{2-36}$$

The roots are given by the equation

$$x_{1,2} = \frac{-b \pm \sqrt{b^2 - 4ac}}{2a} \tag{2-37}$$

In this simple program, we shall assume that $b^2-4ac \geqslant \emptyset$. In Chapter 4 we shall consider procedures that allow us to remove this restriction. The program is

```
PROGRAM QUADRATICROOT(INPUT,OUTPUT);
(*A QUADRATIC EQUATION ROOT CALCULATION*)
VAR A,B,C,INTVAR,ROOT1,ROOT2:REAL;
```

```
BEGIN
   READLN(A);
   READLN(B);                                        (2-38)
   READLN(C);
   INTVAR:=B*B-4.Ø*A*C;
   INTVAR:=SQRT(INTVAR);
   ROOT1:=(-B+INTVAR)/(2.Ø*A);
   ROOT2:=(-B-INTVAR)/(2.Ø*A);
   WRITELN(ROOT1);
   WRITELN(ROOT2);
END.
```

2-6. CONSTANTS

Computer programs often involve some constants which are used repeatedly. For instance, in a simple case, suppose that we were calculating the areas and circumferences of circles. Then, a constant that would be used in each calculation is

$$\pi = 3.14159 \qquad (2\text{-}39)$$

We could just write 3.14159 repeatedly throughout the program. Such a number written explicitly is called a *literal*. Writing literals is often very cumbersome. In PASCAL, a name can replace a literal through the use of a CONST declaration statement, as illustrated in the following program

```
PROGRAM CIRCLE(INPUT,OUTPUT);
(*CALCULATES AREA AND CIRCUMFERENCE OF CIRCLES*)
CONST PI = 3.14159;
VAR RADIUS,CIRCUMFERENCE,AREA:REAL;
BEGIN                                                (2-4Ø)
   READLN(RADIUS);
   CIRCUMFERENCE:=2.Ø*PI*RADIUS;
   AREA:=PI*SQR(RADIUS);
   WRITELN(CIRCUMFERENCE);
   WRITELN(AREA)
END.
```

Several constants can be declared. For instance,

```
CONST RATE1=Ø.Ø9;RATE2=Ø.152;
          RATE3=Ø.268;                               (2-41)
```

(note the semicolons—not commas). In general, the CONST statement *must precede* the VAR declaration.

If an integer is to be declared a constant, then the literal may not have a decimal point. Similarly, a real number must contain a decimal point. Declaring a constant has several advantages over the use of literals. If the constant is used many times, it is clearer and easier to write the constant name. We could avoid the CONST declaration by writing a PASCAL statement such as

```
PI:=3.14159;                                        (2-42)
```

in place of the CONST declaration. However, there are times when we want to run the program with a different value for the constant. Of course we would not, in general, change the value of π. However, consider the interest rates declared in (2-41). If we wanted to change them, and then run the program again, only the CONST declaration need be changed. If literals are used, then many statements of the program would have to be changed. If we used a set of statements such as that of (2-42), it might be possible to miss one of them when the program was changed. Thus, if there are constants used in your program, it is advisable to declare them using a CONST expression.

The CONST expression is more versatile than we have indicated. Constants can be declared as the negative of other constants.

```
CONST MAXIMUM=1.9632714;
      MINIMUM=-MAXIMUM;                             (2-43)
      BIGGEST=+MAXIMUM;
```

It may seem as though the declaration

```
BIGGEST=+MAXIMUM;
```

is unnecessary. However, suppose that you mistakenly used BIGGEST as a constant in one part of your program and MAXIMUM as the same constant in another part of the program. Such a declaration then eliminates the need for rewriting the program. A syntax diagram for CONST is shown in Fig. 2-1.

2-7. THE SYNTAX OF TYPICAL VAR DECLARATIONS

We have used the VAR statement to declare identifiers of the type REAL or INTEGER. There are other declarations that can be used. We shall consider them in subsequent chapters of the book. In this section,

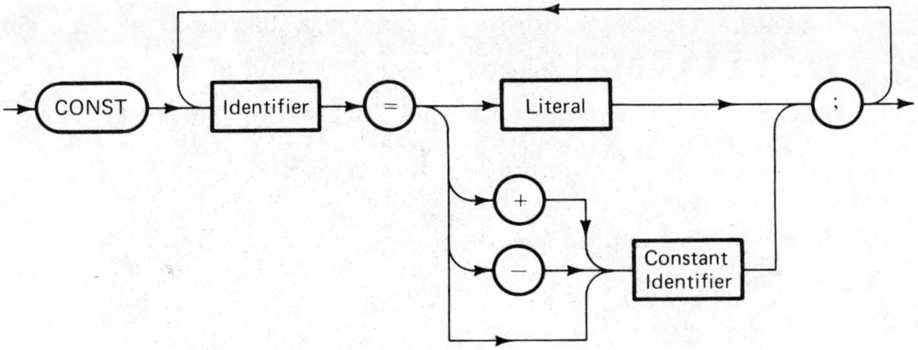

Figure 2-1. Syntax diagram for CONST declaration

for completeness, we formally list the syntax diagram for the VAR declaration, see Fig. 2-2. The only type designations that we have considered are REAL and INTEGER. However there are others such as CHAR, which allow us to work with letters and to perform such operations as simple alphabetization as well as more complex procedures. There is also a type called BOOLEAN, which is used with logical operators. These types will be discussed in Chapters 4 and 6.

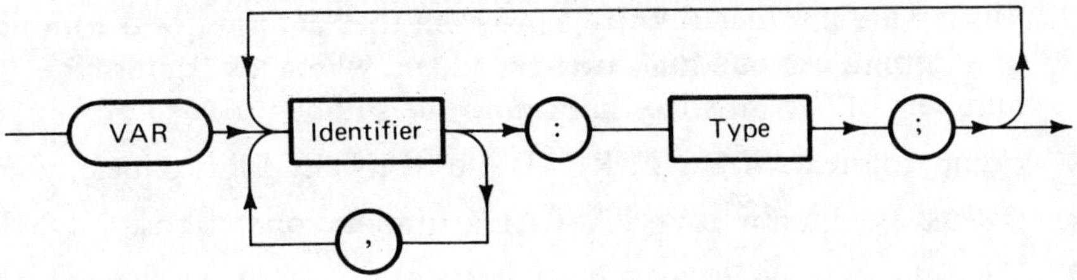

Figure 2-2. Syntax diagram for VAR declaration

EXERCISES

1. Discuss the difference between real numbers and integers.
2. Run a PASCAL program on your computer than computes the algebraic expression

$$x = a + b - cd/2$$

Use the following REAL values: a = 1.23, b = Ø.12E2, c = 2.75, d = 4.32.

3. Repeat Exercise 2 but now use the integer values

   a = 1, b = 2, c = 3, d = 4

4. Describe the final values of X and Y when the following segment of a PASCAL program is evaluated.

```
   ⋮
A:=2;
B:=3;
X:=A+B DIV A;
Y:=B*(B MOD A);
   ⋮
```

5. Repeat Exercise 4 but now use the assignments

```
A:=2;
B:=-3;
```

6. Repeat Exercise 4 but now use the assignments

```
A:=-2;
B:=3;
```

7. The shipping department of a certain company packs 1ØØ bars of soap into a single shipping carton. On a given day NUMBERBARS of soap are produced. Write a program that determines the number of shipping cartons that are needed and which also determines the numbers of bars of soap that cannot be shipped.
8. Compare the accuracy of REAL and of INTEGER numbers.
9. Discuss the hierarchy of PASCAL arithmetic operations.
10. The following values have been assigned in a PASCAL program:

```
A:=2.63;
B:=3.47;
C:=9.31;
D:=2.78;
E:=3.62;
```

   Determine the value of X computed by the following expression

```
X:=A+B*D+D/E+B;
```

11. Repeat Exercise 1Ø for

```
X:=(A+B)*(A/D+E)/E+B;
```

12. Repeat Exercise 1∅ for

```
X:=A+B*(C+D/E*(A+B)/C+D*E)*(A*(C+D*(A+E)));
```

13. The following integer values have been assigned in a PASCAL program

```
A:=1;
B:=2;
C:=3;
D:=4;
E:=–1;
```

Determine the value of the INTEGER computed by the following expression

```
X:=A+B*D+D DIV E+B;
```

14. Repeat Exercise 13 for

```
X:=(A+B*(C+D DIV E)+(A+B MOD C) DIV C)
                    *(A+C DIV E);
```

15. What is meant by a mixed mode operation?
16. Consider the program

```
PROGRAM MIXEDARITH(INPUT,OUTPUT);
VAR I,J,K,L,M,N:INTEGER;
      A,B,C,D,E,F,G:REAL;
BEGIN
   READLN(A);
   READLN(B);
   READLN(C);
   READLN(I);
   READLN(J);
   READLN(K);
   E:=B/C;
   D:=I/J;
   M:= I DIV J;
   G:=D+I/J;
   L:=I–J;
   F:=A+ I MOD J;
   WRITELN(D);
   WRITELN(E);
```

```
    WRITELN(F);
    WRITELN(G);
    WRITELN(L);
    WRITELN(M);
    WRITELN(N);
END.
```

The following data is supplied:

```
A:=1.23; B:=4.56; C:=6.78; I:=4; J:=7; K:=9;
```

What values are output?

17. Repeat Exercise 16 but now use the data

```
A:=-1.23; B:=4.56; C:=6.78; I:=-4; J:=7; K:=9;
```

18. Repeat Exercise 16 but now use the data

```
A:=1.23; B:=4.56; C:=6.78; I:=4; J:=-7; K:=-9;
```

19. Write a PASCAL program that takes the square root of a number. Run the program on your computer.
20. Write a PASCAL program that takes the cube root of a number. Run the program on your computer.
21. Write a PASCAL program that accepts five REAL numbers as data, takes their sum, and then prints the closest integer to the sum.
22. Write a PASCAL program that inputs five REAL numbers and takes their sum. The REAL numbers can have up to 5 significant figures after the decimal point. Print the sum to an accuracy of only two signficant figures.
23. Use trigonometric identities to compute the hypotenuse and other side of a right triangle. The length of one side is 50 meters and the angle is 40° (180° = π radians).
24. Write a PASCAL program to convert from inches to centimeters and from kilometers to miles. Use CONST declarations.

Chapter Three

Input and Output

This chapter deals with the inputting and outputting of data on devices such as the terminal, the card reader, and the line printer. In Chapter 8 we shall discuss the inputting and outputting of data on magnetic disks or tape.

3-1. THE READ AND READLN INSTRUCTIONS

So far, we have used the PASCAL instruction READLN to input a single item of data. We shall now consider some more versatile modifications of this statement. There are actually two forms of input statements, READ and READLN.

Let us consider the READ statement first. Its general form is

```
READ(Identifier1,Identifier2,. . . ,Identifier n);
```
(3-1)

That is, it consists of the keyword READ followed by a list of identifiers which is enclosed in parentheses. The identifiers are separated by commas, although there is no comma after the last one. In accordance with the usual rules of PASCAL, a semicolon has been placed at the end of statement (3-1). As an example, consider

```
READ(NUMBER,TIME,VELOCITY);
```
(3-2)

When the READ statement is executed, values will be assigned to each identifier in the list, provided that the required data is supplied. For instance, in example (3-2), three numbers must be supplied. The numbers must agree with the type of the identifier. Suppose that NUMBER had been declared to be an INTEGER, while TIME and VELOCITY were declared to be REAL. Then, a number with no decimal point must be entered for NUMBER, while numbers with fractional parts would be entered for TIME and VELOCITY.

Now let us consider how the data would be entered. First we shall assume that a terminal is used. Three numbers would be entered. The numbers must be separated by delimiters which can be either spaces between the numbers or (carriage) returns. A return *must* always follow the last item of data. For instance, several ways of entering the same data would be

```
47
2.37    7.28E-1                                  (3-3a)

47      2.37      7.28E-1                        (3-3b)

47
2.37                                             (3-3c)
7.28E-1
```

Note that a (carriage) return always follows the last data item and that there are *no commas written.*

When punch cards are used, the same ideas apply. Each punch card can be viewed as a line on the terminal. Thus, in the previous example, the data could be punched either on a single card or on separate cards. Again, a blank space (or spaces) would be used as a delimiter when more than one item of data is punched on a single card.

Data is always read in order. For instance, with statement (3-2), the value assigned to NUMBER would be the first data encountered, that for TIME would be the second one, etc.

There can be more than one READ statement in a program. For instance,

```
    :
READ(NUMBER,TIME,VELOCITY);
    :                                            (3-4)
READ(GAIN,VOLTAGE,CURRENT);
    :
```

These two READ statements are equivalent to the single statement

```
READ(NUMBER,TIME,VELOCITY,
                  GAIN,VOLTAGE,CURRENT);        (3-5)
```

provided that there are no intervening READ statements. Now six items of data can be entered on one to six lines (or one to six cards). Any extra data (e.g. a seventh item of data written on the terminal or punched on a card) will be ignored.

If there is not enough data, then an error results. This will be treated differently by different computer installations. For instance, if you are inputting data from a terminal, and you do not enter enough data, then the computation will not proceed. Entering successive carriage returns may not produce any action. That is, computation will proceed up to the READ statement in question and then cease until enough data is supplied. If you are running a program in the batch processing mode, computation may cease and an error message will be given. The procedures are not standard and your computer manual should be checked.

There are times when we do no know how much data is to be read. For instance, suppose that we want to write a program for a department store that totals the dollar amount of purchases made by all the customers in a month. However, the number of purchases can vary from customer to customer. Suppose that each individual purchase is punched on a different punch card. It would be cumbersome to have to count the number of cards. There are procedures to allow for variable length READs. We shall discuss them in Section 6-3.

Now let us consider the READLN statement which we have used. Its form is the same as that of the READ statement

```
READLN(Identifier1,Identifier2,. . .,Identifier n);          (3-6)
```

The execution of the READLN statement is essentially the same as that of the READ statement except that any data after that assigned to the last identifier in the list that is typed on the same line, or punched on the same card, will be ignored. For instance, consider the following

```
READLN(A,B,C);
READ(D,E,F,G);
READ(BOX,BOOK);                                               (3-7)
READLN;
READLN(H,I,J,K);
```

Suppose that the following data were entered on separate lines or cards

```
23    4.7    9.37    5.68    7.32
1.67    9.24    −3.21    −17.23    15.34
14.38    15.21    16.73    18.42    19.37
25.6            2.3            37.8            42.7            51.

25.6    2.3    37.8    42.7    51.9    82.3
```

The first three values would be assigned to A, B, and C. That is

```
A:=2.3;
B:=4.7;
C:=9.37;
```

The READLN would then cause the remainder of the data on the first line to be ignored. Hence, when the first READ statement is executed, we assign the following values:

```
D:=1.67;
E:=9.24;
F:=-3.21;
G:=-17.23;
```

The next READ statement causes

```
BOX:=15.34;
BOOK:=14.38;
```

Now consider the READLN statement which comes next. This has no list. However, it does cause skipping to the next line, or next card. Hence, the 15.21, 16.73, 18.42 and 19.37 will be skipped and

```
H:=25.6;
I:=2.3;
J:=37.8;
K:=42.7;
```

The READ statement causes data to be read in the order in which it is entered with no regard to returns (or to new cards). The READLN statement functions in the same way except that *after* a READLN statement is executed, all the remaining data on the current line or card is ignored. For instance, if the first statement is

```
READLN;
```

then the first line (or card) of data will be ignored.

The reader may ask why both READ and READLN statements are necessary. It provides versatility. For instance, suppose that each card contained 5 items of data for a student. The first three items are grades on three tests, the next number is the student ID number, and the last item is the seat number. If we want only to average all the students' test grades, then only the first three items of data on each card need be read. The READLN statement could be used to read three items only and then skip to the next card.

3-2. THE WRITE AND WRITELN STATEMENTS

When we want to output data to the printer or terminal, the WRITE or WRITELN statement is used. If you are inputting data on a terminal, then the output will usually be to the terminal. If you are using batch processing, then the output will usually be to the printer. We shall discuss procedures for modifying this in Sec. 8-5.

Let us start by considering the WRITE statement. Its simplest form is

```
WRITE(Identifier1,Identifier2, . . .,Identifier n);          (3-8)
```

For instance,

```
    :
    .

    :
    .
WRITE(ITEM,VELOCITY,TIME);                                   (3-9)
    :
    .
```

It is assumed that the values of ITEM, VELOCITY, and TIME have been assigned earlier in the program. When the WRITE statement is executed, the numerical values of ITEM, VELOCITY, and TIME will be printed. The form of printing may vary from computer to computer. In general, a given number of columns called a *field width* is used to print each number. The field width for INTEGERS is different than that for REAL variables. For instance, suppose that ITEM is an INTEGER and that VELOCITY and TIME are REAL. In addition, their values are:

```
ITEM:=5317;
VELOCITY:=-2.3Ø16E+3;
TIME:=1.2347E+1Ø;
```

On some large computers, the field width for integers is 1Ø spaces and that for real numbers is 22 spaces. The output would appear as

```
bbbbbb5317b-2.3Ø16ØØØØØØØØE+ØØ3bb1.2347ØØØØØØØØE+Ø1Ø
```

(where the b's represent blank spaces). On some smaller computers, the result might appear as

```
5317b-2.3Ø16E3b1.2347E1Ø
```

We shall consider procedures whereby the programmer can control the field width in the next section. The output of a WRITE statement will be printed on a single line if there is enough room.

The data resulting from a sequence of WRITE statements will also be printed on a single line if there is enough room. For instance, the following statements will cause output which is equivalent to that caused by statement (3-9)

```
WRITE(ITEM,VELOCITY);
   .
   .                                        (3-1Øa)
   .
WRITE(TIME);
```

The following three statements will also produce output which is equivalent to that produced by statement (3-9).

```
WRITE(ITEM);
WRITE(VELOCITY);                            (3-1Øb)
WRITE(TIME);
```

Actually, the WRITE statement causes the data which is to be printed to be stored in a set of memory locations which is called a *buffer*. On some computers, the contents of the buffer will not be printed until the buffer is filled or until a carriage return command is given.

When the contents of the buffer is printed, the buffer is emptied (set equal to blanks) and then more data can be supplied to it. For instance, in (3-9), (3-1Øa) or (3-1Øb) the data might not be printed until the buffer was filled. This problem can be avoided by using the WRITELN statement, since this automatically returns the carriage after the list has been written. That is, the WRITELN statement is essentially the same as the WRITE statement except that, after all the data in its list is written to the buffer, a carriage return is generated. This causes the present contents of the buffer to be printed on a single line if enough space is available. If a printer is used, the paper is advanced one line; if a terminal is used, the equivalent occurs and subsequent data will be printed on the next line. The general form of the WRITELN statement is

```
WRITELN(Identifier1,Identifier2,. . .,Identifier n);     (3-11)
```

Let us illustrate the use of the WRITELN with the following example

```
   .
   .
   .
WRITE(A,B);
   .
   .
   .
```

```
        WRITE(C);                                    (3-12)
        WRITELN(D,E);
            .
            .
            .
        WRITE(F);
        WRITELN(G,H);
            .
            .
            .
        WRITE(I);
            .
            .
            .
        WRITELN;
```

Now the values of A, B, C, D, and E will be printed on the first line (if there is enough room). The next two statements then cause the value of F to be printed on the second line along with the values of G and H. The value of I will then be printed on the next line. Note the WRITELN at the end of the list. If it were not present then the value of I might (depending on the computer) remain in the buffer and not be printed. The last WRITELN forces the printing of I since the buffer will be emptied and the paper advanced one line.

If a WRITELN or WRITE statement has a long list of variables to be printed, then it is possible that all of the data may not fit on a single line. In such cases, the results will vary from computer to computer. In some cases a new line will be started automatically. However, your computer manual should be checked to determine the results of such an operation.

3-3. THE FORMAT OF NUMERICAL OUTPUT

The procedures using the WRITE or the WRITELN discussed in the last section provided no control over the form of the output. For instance, depending upon the computer installation, all REAL data may be printed with 22 decimal places. We also have no control over where on the line the data is printed. However, PASCAL does provide a procedure whereby the form of the output data can be varied. This is called *formatting* the output data.

To control the spacing of data, each piece of data can be printed in a specified *field.* A field designates a number of columns. For instance, suppose that we have the INTEGERS

```
I:=346;
J:=17865;
```

If we specify that I is to be printed in a field of 1Ø characters, and that J is to be printed in a field of 8 characters, then the resulting output would appear as

```
bbbbbbb346bbb17865
```

where the b's are blank spaces. The data is always moved over to the right edge of the field. It is said to be *right adjusted* or *right justified*. If you specify too small a field, then the field specifier will be "expanded" by the computer to fit the output. In such cases, the spacing may not be of the desired form.

In PASCAL, the field width is specified by a colon followed by a number which is written to the right of the identifier in the WRITE or WRITELN statement. For instance, for the previous example, we would write

```
WRITE(I:1Ø,J:8);                                (3-13)
```

When we deal with REAL data, then we can specify both the field width and the number of decimal places by using a second colon and number. For instance, suppose that I and J are declared as INTEGER and VEL and TIME are declared as REAL. Then,

```
WRITE(I:1Ø,VEL:8:2,TIME:12:4,J:6);              (3-14)
```

would cause the value of I to be written in the first 1Ø columns, the value of VEL to be written in the next 8 columns using 2 decimal places, the value of TIME to be written in the next 12 columns using four places following the decimal point, and the value of the integer J will be written in the next 6 columns. For instance, if we have

```
I:=2364;
J:=172;
VEL:=176.345
TIME:=1837.2386;
```

then the resulting output would be

```
bbbbbb2364bb176.35bbb1837.2386bbb172
```

Remember that if you do not specify a large enough field, then the field will be expanded by the computer, which may reduce the readability of your output. If a REAL number becomes large enough so that E notation is required, then the decimal specifier may be ignored by the computer.

3-4. PRINTING OF TEXT WITH OUTPUT

Thus far we have only considered the printing of numerical data. However, it often would make the output far more readable and meaningful if appropriate text material could also be printed. In this section we shall consider some procedures for doing just this.

Text material can be printed by placing it within the parentheses of a WRITE or WRITELN statement. All such text should be enclosed in single quotes. For instance,

```
WRITELN(' ANSWERS ARE');                                (3-15)
```

would result in

```
ANSWERS ARE
```

being printed.

Text can be interspersed with variables in a WRITE or WRITELN statement.

```
WRITELN(' VELOCITY=',VEL,'TIME=',TIME);                 (3-16)
```

For instance if, earlier in the program, we had computed

```
VEL:=2.3456E2;
TIME:=2.54567E3;
```

then, assuming that REAL data is printed with five digits after the decimal point, the output would be

```
VELOCITY=2.3456E2TIME=2.54567E3                         (3-17)
```

Note that, naturally, if your computer prints more places for REAL variables, then they would be printed here.

The spacing of the printed material in (3-17) should be modified to make it more readable. One procedure for doing this is to include additional spaces within the quotes. For instance,

```
WRITELN(' VELOCITY=',VEL,'    TIME=',TIME);             (3-18)
```

would cause four spaces to be included to the left of the word TIME, resulting in a more readable output.

Field width specifiers can be used with text material to control spacing. For instance, we could modify statement (3-16) in the following way.

```
WRITELN(' VELOCITY=':15,VEL:10:2,
        'TIME=':7,TIME:8:2);                    (3-19)
```

Now the word and symbol VELOCITY= will be right adjusted in a field of 15 columns and the word and symbol TIME= will be printed right adjusted in a field of 7 columns, and the output will appear as

```
bbbbbbVELOCITY=bbbb234.56bbTIME=bb254.57       (3-20)
```

Note that we have always used a blank space as the first character printed on a line (after the first quote). On many, but not all, computers this first character is *not* printed, but is used as a *carriage control character*. That is, it controls the spacing between lines. Typically, if the first character is a blank, then the printer will be advanced one line before printing. This is ordinary single spacing. That is, suppose that a previous WRITELN caused data to be printed. Now the paper is advanced one line and the new data is printed. If the first character is a Ø, double spacing results. Table 3-1 lists the common carriage control characters used in PASCAL.

TABLE 3-1. CARRIAGE CONTROL CHARACTERS

Symbol	*Action*
blank space	advance one line before printing
Ø	advance two lines before printing
1	skip to top of next page before printing
+	do not advance (will overprint)

Remember that carriage control characters are not standard and not all computers use them.

Printing of Prompt Messages to be Used with READ Statements

Printing of text can be very helpful when data is entered on a terminal. For instance, in the programs we have written thus far, operation proceeds until the data has to be entered. However, the person running the program has to know what data is to be entered, and in what order and form, and the appropriate printing of text can prompt him. For instance, let us modify program (2-38) to include such prompting. We shall also use text for output printing.

```
PROGRAM QUADRATICROOT(INPUT,OUTPUT);
(*QUADRATIC ROOT CALCULATION*)
VAR A,B,C,INTVAR,ROOT1,ROOT2:REAL;
BEGIN
   WRITELN(' THE QUADRATIC IS A*X*X+B*X+C');
   WRITELN(' ENTER A,B, AND C');                    (3-21)
   READLN(A,B,C);
   WRITELN(' A=',A,'B=',B,'C=',C);
   INTVAR:=B*B-4.Ø*A*C);
   INTVAR:=SQRT(INTVAR);
   ROOT1:=(-B+INTVAR)/(2.Ø*A);
   ROOT2:=(-B-INTVAR)/(2.Ø*A);
   WRITELN(' ONE ROOT =',ROOT1);
   WRITELN(' ANOTHER ROOT =',ROOT2);
END.
```

Now the user knows exactly what data to enter and in what order. The output is identified. Note the line that prints the values of A, B, and C. It is good practice to print the input data as a check. In this way, the person using the program can verify if the data has been correctly entered. Remember that this program only works if B*B–4.Ø*A*C is not negative. In the next chapter we shall consider procedures for overcoming this limitation.

EXERCISES

1. Discuss the operation of the following statement

   ```
   READ(VARIABLE,SPEED,VELOCITY,BOX);
   ```

2. For the statement of Exercise 1, the data is in the form

   ```
   15    13.27    15.234E3    23    14.23E6
   ```

   What values will be assigned to the variables?

3. Repeat Exercise 2 but now assume that the data is in the form

   ```
   15    13.27
   15.234E3
   23    14.23E6
   ```

4. Assuming that the data of Exercise 2 (or 3) is correct, identify which variables of Exercise 1 are REAL and which are INTEGER.

5. For the following sequence of statements

```
READ(ITEM,VELOCITY,TIME);
READ(DATA,DAY);
```

the following data is supplied

```
14     26.37    15.8    17.3
24.63    2    7
```

What values are assigned to the variables?

6. Repeat Exercise 4 but now assume that the data is in the following form:

```
14    26.37
15.8    17.3
24.63    2    7
```

7. Repeat Exercise 5 but now assume that the first READ statement is replaced by a READLN statement.

8. Repeat Exercise 6 but now assume that the first READ statement is replaced by a READLN statement.

9. Repeat Exercise 5 but now assume that both READ statements are replaced by READLN statements.

1Ø. For the following sequence of statements

```
READLN(A,B,C);
READ(D,E,F,G,H);
READ(I);
READLN(J,K,L);
READ(M);
READLN(N);
```

the following data is supplied

```
23.4    15.6    17.3    18.9    17.2    26.7    34.8
19.6    23.7
17.8    14.9    19.3    46.87    54.23
1Ø1.Ø1    14E3    17.Ø1    19.23    79.23    67.38
48.37    54.32    81.78    9Ø.23    1Ø1.46
256.37    72.48    96.375    156.8
```

```
192.3    174.37    1Ø8.26
```

What values are assigned to the variables?

11. Repeat Exercise 1Ø but assume that the first READ statement is replaced by a READLN statement.

12. Repeat Exercise 11 but now assume that a statement

```
READLN;
```

is included at the start of the program.

13. Discuss the output that results when the following sequence of statements is executed.

```
TIME:=17.3E2;
VELOCITY:=19.43617E3;
ITEM:=94;
NUMBER:=78;
WRITELN(ITEM,VELOCITY,NUMBER,TIME);
```

14. Repeat Exercise 13 but now replace the last statement with

```
WRITE(ITEM,VELOCITY);
WRITE(NUMBER,TIME);
WRITELN;
```

15. Repeat Exercise 13 but now replace the last statement with

```
WRITE(ITEM,VELOCITY);
WRITELN(NUMBER);
WRITELN(TIME);
```

16. Repeat Exercise 13 but now use

```
WRITELN(ITEM:4,VELOCITY:15:3,NUMBER:6,
                              TIME:1Ø:2);
```

17. Repeat Exercise 13 but now use

```
WRITE(ITEM:4,VELOCITY:15:3);
WRITE(NUMBER:6,TIME:1Ø:2);
WRITELN;
```

18. Repeat Exercise 13 but now use

```
WRITELN(' ITEM NUMB=',ITEM:4,'VELOCITY=',
           VELOCITY:5:3,'NUMBER=',NUMBER:6,
           'ELAPSED TIME=',TIME:1Ø:2);
```

19. Repeat Exercise 13 but now use

```
WRITELN(' ITEM NUMB=',ITEM:4,'VELOCITY=':12,
        VELOCITY:5:3,'NUMBER=':10,NUMBER:6,
        'ELAPSED TIME=':15,TIME:10:2);
```

20. Modify your program of Exercise 2-19 to include appropriate printing of text with the output. The input data should also be checked. If the program is to be run from a terminal, then appropriate prompting should also be included.

21. Repeat Exercise 20 for the program of Exercise 2-20.

22. Repeat Exercise 20 for the program of Exercise 2-7.

23. Repeat Exercise 20 for the program of Exercise 2-21.

24. Repeat Exercise 20 for the program of Exercise 2-22.

25. Repeat Exercise 20 for the program of Exercise 2-23.

26. Repeat Exercise 20 for the program of Exercise 2-24.

Chapter Four

Control Statements—Basic Ideas of Structured Programming

We have thus far considered PASCAL programs that executed each statement in order. Actually, such programs are of limited use, and far more powerful programs can be written if there are several possible branches or paths available. The computer then chooses the branch to take depending upon some programmed decision-making process. For instance, consider program (2-28) which could only evaluate the roots of a quadratic if b^2-4ac was positive. If the program had two branches, one which calculated SQRT(B*B–4.Ø*A*C) and the other which calculated SQRT(4.Ø*A*C–B*B), this problem would be avoided. We shall consider procedures for such branching in this chapter.

There are also times when it is desirable for a program to "loop back" over a set of statements a number of times. We shall also discuss procedures which allow such looping in this chapter.

If branching and looping can be used, then much more complex algorithms can be written which, in turn, results in more complex programs. There are procedures that can be used for writing these complex programs that make them much less error-prone and much easier to debug. The techniques for writing such programs are referred to as *structured programming*. We shall discuss its basic elements in this chapter.

4-1. BOOLEAN VARIABLES—CONDITIONS

We have discussed REAL and INTEGER variables that were numbers. PASCAL also has other forms of variables. One is the *BOOLEAN variable* which is named for the logician George Boole. The BOOLEAN variable can take on only one of two values, TRUE or FALSE. A variable can be declared BOOLEAN in the VAR statement. For instance,

```
VAR ITEM,NUMBER:INTEGER;
    VELOCITY,SPEED,TIME,HEIGHT:REAL;          (4-1)
    POSITIVE,BIGGEST,TEST:BOOLEAN;
```

It may seem strange to have variables that can only be TRUE or FALSE. However, we shall demonstrate in this chapter how they can be used in various decision-making processes.

Let us demonstrate some valid BOOLEAN expressions. Some simple ones are

```
BIGGEST:=TRUE;                                (4-2a)
POSITIVE:=FALSE;                              (4-2b)
```

That is, we can use an assignment statement to declare a BOOLEAN variable to be either TRUE or FALSE or to be the same as another BOOLEAN variable. Some, but not all, computers allow the printing of BOOLEAN variables. For instance, the following statement

```
WRITELN(TEST);                                (4-3)
```

results in either the word TRUE or the word FALSE being printed. In general, BOOLEAN variables cannot be used with READ or READLN statements. The main use for BOOLEAN statements comes about in the procedures to be discussed in the remainder of this chapter.

The BOOLEAN variable is more versatile than we have indicated. For instance, suppose that we have the declaration of (4-1). Then, some valid PASCAL statements are

```
POSITIVE:=VELOCITY>SPEED;                     (4-4)
TEST:=ITEM=NUMBER;                            (4-5)
```

Statement (4-4) means the following: If the number assigned to VELOCITY is greater than the number assigned to SPEED, then POSITIVE will be assigned the value TRUE; otherwise it will be assigned FALSE. Similarly, statement (4-5) assigns the value TRUE to TEST if the value assigned to ITEM is exactly equal to the value assigned to NUMBER; otherwise TEST will be FALSE. (Note the use of the = without the colon in (4-5).)

The symbols = and > are called *relational operators*. In Table 4-1 we list all of these which are used in PASCAL.

TABLE 4-1. RELATIONAL OPERATORS

Operator	*Meaning*
=	Equal
>	Greater than
<	Less than
>=	Greater than or equal to
<=	Less than or equal to
<>	Not equal to

For instance,

```
TEST:=A<>B;
```
(4-6)

assigns TRUE to TEST if A is not equal to B and assigns FALSE to TEST if A and B are equal. It is assumed that A and B are either both of type REAL or both INTEGER and that TEST is of type BOOLEAN. In a subsequent chapter we shall discuss that A and B can be variables of other types.

Care should be taken when the = relational operator is used. For instance,

```
TEST:=VELOCITY=SPEED;
```
(4-7)

Suppose that VELOCITY and SPEED are real variables which have been computed previously in the program. Then, roundoff error may cause them to be unequal even though they should be equal. For instance, suppose that we *should* have VELOCITY and SPEED both assigned the value 5.Ø (exactly). Because of roundoff, VELOCITY may be assigned the value 5.ØØØØ1 and SPEED may be assigned the value 4.99999. In such a case, we want TEST to be assigned the value TRUE. However, this will *not* be done and FALSE will be assigned, and an undesirable situation has resulted. We could avoid this by replacing statement (4-7) with a statement such as

```
TEST:=ABS(VELOCITY-SPEED)<Ø.ØØØ1
```
(4-8)

Now TEST will be TRUE if the difference between VELOCITY and SPEED is less than Ø.ØØØ1. The above discussed problem will not exist with INTEGER variables since roundoff error does not result.

Logical Operators

There are other operators called *logical operators* that can be used with BOOLEAN variables, for instance,

```
TEST:=BOOL1 AND BOOL2;
```
(4-9)

where TEST, BOOL1 and BOOL2 are BOOLEAN variables. TEST will be TRUE if both BOOL1 *and* BOOL2 are TRUE. If either BOOL1 or BOOL2 or both are FALSE, then TEST is FALSE. AND is called a *logical operator*. Table 4-2 lists those logical operators used in PASCAL.

TABLE 4-2. LOGICAL OPERATORS

Operator	*Meaning*
BOOL1 AND BOOL2	TRUE if both BOOL1 and BOOL2 are TRUE FALSE if either BOOL1 or BOOL2 or both are FALSE
BOOL1 OR BOOL2	TRUE if either BOOL1 or BOOL2 or both are TRUE FALSE only if both BOOL1 and BOOL2 are FALSE
NOT BOOL1	TRUE if BOOL1 is FALSE FALSE IF BOOL1 is TRUE

The BOOLEAN variables to the right of the assignment sign in (4-9) can be replaced by PASCAL expressions using relational operators. For instance,

```
BOOL:=(A>B)OR(ITEM=NUMBER);
```
(4-10)

where BOOL must be of type BOOLEAN and, for example, A and B are REAL and ITEM and NUMBER are INTEGER. Then BOOL will be TRUE if A is greater than B or if ITEM is equal to NUMBER or if both A is greater than B and ITEM is equal to NUMBER.

A more complex statement is

```
BOOL:=((A>B)OR(ITEM=NUMBER))AND(I=J);
```
(4-11)

This will be TRUE if I=J *and* either A>B *or* ITEM=NUMBER *or* if I=J and both A>B and ITEM=NUMBER.

There is a hierarchy of logical and relational operations that is combined with the arithmetic hierarchy. However, as in the case of arithmetic operations, parentheses can be used to override the hierarchy. The overall hierarchy of logical and arithmetic operations is summarized in the following table.

TABLE 4-3. HIERARCHIES

NOT negation	highest
* / DIV MOD AND	↓
+ − OR	↓
<= >= = <>	lowest

All items on the same line are on the same level of hierarchy. That is, the PASCAL operation is scanned from left to right. First all NOT and negation operations are performed; next multiplication, division, MOD and AND operations are performed. Finally, the relational operations are performed. Remember that parentheses can be used to modify the hierarchy. For instance, in statements (4-10) and (4-11), the parentheses around A>B, I=J, and ITEM=NUMBER are required to cause the relational operations to be performed before the logical ones.

Let us consider some examples of hierarchy. The following pairs of statements are equivalent.

```
BOOL:=((A+B)=(C+D))AND BOOL1 OR BOOL2;      (4-12a)
BOOL:=(((A+B)=(C+D))AND BOOL1)OR BOOL2;     (4-12b)
```

where BOOL, BOOL1 and BOOL2 are of type BOOLEAN and all other variables are of type INTEGER. As another example, consider

```
BOOL:=BOOL1 OR BOOL2 AND BOOL3;             (4-13a)
BOOL:=BOOL1 OR (BOOL2 AND BOOL3);           (4-13b)
```

Another pair of equivalent expressions is

```
BOOL:=BOOL1 OR NOT BOOL2 AND BOOL3;         (4-14a)
BOOL:=BOOL1 OR ((NOT BOOL2)AND BOOL3);      (4-14b)
```

In the next section we shall use BOOLEAN variables in decision-making processes.

4-2. THE IF STATEMENT

Now let us consider a statement that allows us to perform decision-making operations. In its simplest form, it is

```
IF(BOOLEAN statement)THEN(statement);                    (4-15)
```

If the BOOLEAN statement is TRUE, then the statement will be executed. If the BOOLEAN statement is FALSE, then the statement will not be executed. For instance,

```
IF (A>B)THEN TIME:=TIME+ELAPSEDTIME;                     (4-16)
```

causes the following to occur. If the value assigned to A is greater than that assigned to B, then the statement TIME:=TIME+ELAPSEDTIME will be executed. If A is equal to or less than B, then the statement TIME:=TIME+ELAPSEDTIME will be skipped.

Let us illustrate this by writing a PASCAL program that inputs three variables and then prints out the maximum entered value.

```
PROGRAM MAXIMUM(INPUT,OUTPUT);                           (4-17a)
(*PROGRAM OBTAINS MAXIMUM OF
                          THREE VARIABLES*)              (4-17b)
VAR INP1,INP2,INP3,MAXIMUM:REAL;                         (4-17c)
BEGIN                                                    (4-17d)
   READ(INP1,INP2,INP3);                                 (4-17e)
   MAXIMUM:=INP1;                                        (4-17f)
   IF(INP2>MAXIMUM)THEN MAXIMUM:=INP2;                   (4-17g)
   IF(INP3>MAXIMUM)THEN MAXIMUM:=INP3;                   (4-17h)
   WRITELN(' THE MAXIMUM VALUE IS',MAXIMUM)              (4-17i)
END.                                                     (4-17j)
```

This program functions in the following way. First, MAXIMUM is set equal to INP1. Now consider statement (4-17g). If INP2 is greater than MAXIMUM, then the old value of MAXIMUM is replaced by the value of INP2; otherwise the value of MAXIMUM remains that of INP1. Hence, after statement (4-17g) is executed, the value assigned to MAXIMUM will be the larger of INP1 and INP2. Similarly, after statement (4-17h) is executed, MAXIMUM will equal the largest input.

The IF statement is more versatile that we have indicated. It can also be written in the following way.

```
IF(BOOLEAN statement)THEN(statement 1)ELSE
                          (statement 2);                 (4-18)
```

If the BOOLEAN statement is TRUE, then statement 1 will be executed and statement 2 will be ignored. If the BOOLEAN statement is FALSE, then statement 2 will be executed and statement 1 will be ignored. A syntax diagram for this IF statement is shown in Fig. 4-1. As an exam-

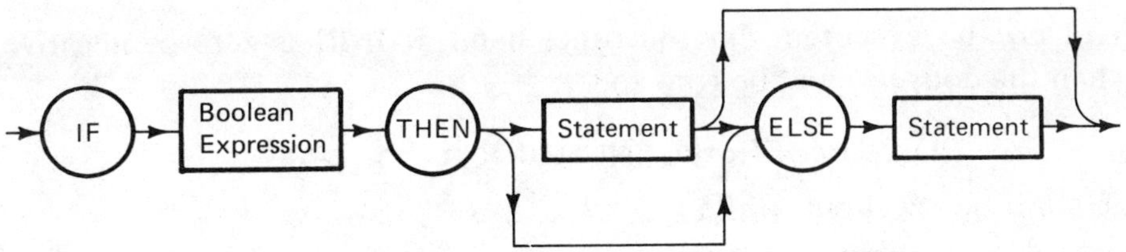

Figure 4-1. Syntax diagram for the IF-THEN-ELSE form

ple, let us write a program that inputs three variables and determines the number of positive values and the number of negative or zero values.

```
PROGRAM POSNEGZERCOUNT(INPUT,OUTPUT);
(*PROGRAM COUNTS NUMBER OF POSITIVE AND NUMBER
                          OF NEGATIVE OR ZERO VALUES*)
VAR INP1,INP2,INP3:REAL;
    POSNUMBER,NEGZERNUMBER:INTEGER;
BEGIN
  POSNUMBER:=Ø;
  NEGZERNUMBER:=Ø;                                    (4-19)
  READLN(INP1,INP2,INP3);
  IF INP1>Ø THEN POSNUMBER:=POSNUMBER+1
           ELSE NEGZERNUMBER:=NEGZERNUMBER+1;
  IF INP2>Ø THEN POSNUMBER:=POSNUMBER+1
           ELSE NEGZERNUMBER:=NEGZERNUMBER+1;
  IF INP3>Ø THEN POSNUMBER:=POSNUMBER+1
           ELSE NEGZERNUMBER:=NEGZERNUMBER+1;
  WRITELN(' THE NUMBER OF POSITIVE INPUTS=',
                          POSNUMBER);
  WRITELN(' THE NUMBER OF NEGATIVE OR ZERO INPUTS=',
                          NEGZERNUMBER)
END.
```

We start by setting two INTEGER variables, POSNUMBER and NEGZERNUMBER equal to zero. Now consider the first IF statement. If INP1 is positive, then the statement

```
POSNUMBER:=POSNUMBER+1
```

will be executed and the statement

```
NEGZERNUMBER:=NEGZERNUMBER+1;
```

will not be executed. On the other hand, if INP1 is zero or negative, then the converse will be true and

```
POSNUMBER:=POSNUMBER+1
```

will not be executed, while

```
NEGZERNUMBER:=NEGZERNUMBER+1;
```

will be executed. Each succeeding IF statement then causes either POSNUMBER or NEGZERNUMBER to be incremented by 1. Hence, when the program is completed, the desired counts will be obtained.

We have illustrated the IF statement with a single statement following the words THEN and ELSE. Actually, these can be compound PASCAL statements. A compound PASCAL statement is written using the words BEGIN and END, see programs (1-4), (1-13) and (1-14). This makes the IF statement much more versatile since it now can be used to choose between two branches of a program. To illustrate the use of compound statements, let us again consider program (2-38) which obtained the roots of the quadratic equation

$$ax^2 + bx + c = \emptyset \tag{4-2\emptyset}$$

The prevous program could only function if $b^2-4ac \geqslant \emptyset$ since, in PASCAL, we cannot take the square root of a negative number. We shall use the IF statement to surmount this difficulty. First let us introduce some notation. In mathematics $\sqrt{-1}$ is written as i, so that if b^2-4ac is negative, we would write

$$\sqrt{b^2 - 4ac} = i\sqrt{4ac - b^2} \tag{4-21}$$

Now consider the program

```
PROGRAM QUADRATICROOTS(INPUT,OUTPUT);
(*QUADRATIC ROOT CALCULATION*)
VAR A,B,C,INTVAR,ROOT1,ROOT2:REAL;
BEGIN
   READLN(A,B,C);
   INTVAR:=B*B-4.Ø*A*C;
   IF INTVAR>=Ø THEN
      BEGIN
        INTVAR:=SQRT(INTVAR);
        ROOT1:=(-B+INTVAR)/(2.Ø*A);                    (4-22)
        ROOT2:=(-B-INTVAR)/(2.Ø*A);
        WRITELN(' ROOTS ARE',ROOT1,'AND',ROOT2);
```

```
          END
        ELSE
          BEGIN
           INTVAR:=-INTVAR;
           INTVAR:=SQRT(INTVAR)/(2.Ø*A);
           B:=-B/(2.Ø*A);
           WRITELN(' ROOTS ARE',B,'+ OR -I',INTVAR);
          END;
      END.
```

If INTVAR is equal to or greater than Ø, then the first branch is calculated and ROOT1 and ROOT2 are calculated, the results are printed and the program skips to the end of the ELSE branch, which in this case is the end of the program. On the other hand, if INTVAR is negative, then the statements between BEGIN and ELSE are skipped and the other branch of the program is computed. INTVAR is replaced by its negative, becoming a positive number so that its square root can be calculated. When the roots are printed in this branch, the letter I is also printed to indicate that the square root of a negative number has been taken. Note that there is no semicolon between the END statement that precedes the ELSE and the ELSE statement. This is important. Since there is no PASCAL statement that begins with ELSE, it would be wrong to place a semicolon there.

There can be IF statements nested within other IF statements. For instance, suppose that we modify program (4-2Ø) so that it prints the number of positive inputs, the number of negative inputs, and the number of zero inputs. The program now becomes

```
PROGRAM POSNEGZERCOUNT(INPUT,OUTPUT);
(*COUNT OF NUMBER OF POSITIVE VALUES, NUMBER OF
      NEGATIVE VALUES AND NUMBER OF ZERO VALUES*)
VAR INP1,INP2,INP3:REAL;
    POSNUMBER,NEGNUMBER,ZERNUMBER:INTEGER;
BEGIN
  POSNUMBER:=Ø;
  NEGNUMBER:=Ø;
  ZERNUMBER:=Ø;                                        (4-23)
  READLN(INP1,INP2,INP3);
  IF INP1=Ø THEN ZERNUMBER:=ZERNUMBER+1
    ELSE IF INP1>Ø THEN POSNUMBER:=POSNUMBER+1
     ELSE NEGNUMBER:=NEGNUMBER+1;
```

```
    IF INP2=Ø THEN ZERNUMBER:=ZERNUMBER+1
      ELSE IF INP2>Ø THEN POSNUMBER:=POSNUMBER+1
        ELSE NEGNUMBER:=NEGNUMBER+1;
    IF INP3=Ø THEN ZERNUMBER:=ZERNUMBER+1
      ELSE IF INP3>Ø THEN POSNUMBER:=POSNUMBER+1
        ELSE NEGNUMBER:=NEGNUMBER+1;
    WRITELN(' NUMBER OF ZERO INPUTS=',ZERNUMBER);
    WRITELN(' NUMBER OF POSITIVE INPUTS=',POSNUMBER);
    WRITELN(' NUMBER OF NEGATIVE INPUTS=',NEGNUMBER);
END.
```

Consider the first IF statement. If INP1=Ø then ZERNUMBER is incremented by 1 and control skips to the second IF statement (the one that begins IF INP2 . . .). On the other hand, if INP1 is not equal to zero, then control skips to the ELSE part of the first IF statement. Now if INP1>Ø is TRUE, then POSNUMBER is incremented by one. On the other hand, if INP1>Ø is FALSE, then NEGNUMBER is incremented by one. Proceeding in this way, the desired counts are obtained.

With nested IF statements, it may be difficult to determine to which IF statement an ELSE belongs. The ELSE belongs to the nearest preceding IF statement provided that there is no other intervening ELSE. That is, we start from the innermost IF and ELSE. They are paired. Then, ignoring these, we take the next innermost IF and ELSE and pair them, continuing in this way until all the IF and ELSE statements are paired.

An IF statement can be written with nothing following the THEN. For instance,

```
IF(A>Ø)THEN
   ELSE B:=B+1;                                   (4-24a)
```

is equivalent to

```
IF(A<=Ø)THEN B:=B+1;                              (4-24b)
```

or to

```
IF NOT(A>Ø)THEN B:=B+1;                           (4-24c)
```

Some of the programs that were written in this section are cumbersome due to the fact that similar statements were written repeatedly. In the subsequent sections of this chapter we shall consider procedures for eliminating such repetition.

4-3. UNCONDITIONAL LOOPING

There are times when we want a program to repeat certain steps several times. Consider program (4-23) of the last section. The IF statements had to be repeated for each variable. Such repetition makes for long programs and tedious programming. In PASCAL there are procedures whereby a program can be made to loop back over certain statements thus avoiding these difficulties. In this section we shall discuss some elementary forms of this kind of looping.

An example of a program segment that results in looping is

```
FOR I:=1 TO 10 DO
   BEGIN
                      }  PASCAL compound statement        (4-25)
   END;
 .
 .
 .
```

It has been assumed that I has been declared an INTEGER variable. (We shall modify this in Sec. 8-1.) The program will then execute the PASCAL compound statements using the value I=1. Then it will again evaluate the compound statements using the value I=2. This process will repeat for 1Ø cycles, that is, for the values I=1, 2, 3, ..., 1Ø. The variable I is called the *index* of the DO loop. For each cycle of the loop, I is incremented by 1.

To illustrate how this looping is used, let us rewrite program (4-23), but now inputting 1Ø variables.

```
PROGRAM POSNEGZERCOUNT(INPUT,OUTPUT);
(*COUNT OF POSITIVE,NEGATIVE, AND ZERO VALUES*)
VAR INP:REAL;
      POSNUMBER,NEGNUMBER,ZERNUMBER,COUNT:REAL;
BEGIN
   POSNUMBER:=Ø;
   NEGNUMBER:=Ø;
   ZERNUMBER:=Ø;                                        (4-26)
   FOR COUNT;=1 TO 1Ø DO
      BEGIN
```

```
            READLN(INP);
            IF INP=Ø THEN ZERNUMBER:=ZERNUMBER+1
              ELSE IF INP>Ø THEN POSNUMBER:=POSNUMBER+1
                ELSE NEGNUMBER:=NEGNUMBER+1;
          END;
      WRITELN(' NUMBER OF ZERO INPUTS',ZERNUMBER);
      WRITELN(' NUMBER OF POSITIVE INPUTS',POSNUMBER);
      WRITELN(' NUMBER OF NEGATIVE INPUTS',NEGNUMBER)
    END.
```

Note the semicolon after the first END. It is required to separate the END from the WRITELN statement.

Program (4-26) did not calculate any value using the index COUNT. It was only used to keep count of th number of times that the loop was cycled. However, the index can be used in calculations. For instance, consider the program segment

```
      :
    BOX:=Ø;
    FOR NUMB:=1 TO 15 DO
      BEGIN
        A:=NUMB*ITEM;                                   (4-27)
        BOX:=BOX+A;
      END;
      :
```

It is assumed that all variables have been appropriately declared in the VAR statement and that the value of NUMB has been assigned earlier in the program.

In the previous examples, the value of the index has been incremented by 1 each time that the loop is cycled. If the word TO is replaced by the word DOWNTO, then *the index will be decremented by 1*. For instance,

```
    FOR COUNT:=1Ø DOWNTO -5 DO
    BEGIN                                               (4-28)
      :
    END;
```

Now the loop will be cycled for COUNT = 1Ø, 9, 8, . . . , Ø, −1, −2, . . . , −5.

A syntax diagram for the looping discussed here is given in Fig. 4-2.

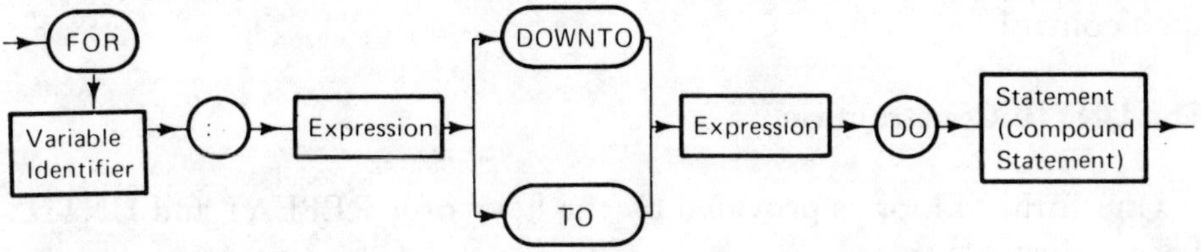

Figure 4-2. Syntax diagram for unconditional looping

This diagram indicates a somewhat more general form than we have used thus far. For instance, we can write

```
FOR I1:=I2 TO I3 DO                          (4-29a)
```

or

```
FOR I1:=I2 DOWNTO I3 DO                      (4-29b)
```

where I2 and I3 can be integers, integer variables, or simple integer expressions. Some valid statements are

```
FOR ITEM:=NUMB TO 1Ø DO                      (4-3Øa)
FOR ITEM:=NUMB1+NUMB2 DOWNTO
                  NUMB3 DO                   (4-3Øb)
```

In expressions (4-29), I2 and I3 are called the *initial value* and *final value*, respectively. The rule in a FOR-TO expression is that the index starts at the initial value and is incremented by 1. The final pass through the loop occurs when the index equals the final value. The same rule applies for the DOWNTO case except that the index is decremented by 1 for each pass through the loop. If, for any reason, the initial value is greater than the final value for the TO case (or if the initial value is less than the final value for the DOWNTO case) then the (compound) statement of the loop will not be executed.

It is not proper PASCAL programming to use the index subsequently in the program. In fact, different PASCAL compilers will produce different results if this is done. Note that statements within the body of the loop *must not* change the index, initial value, or final value.

4-4. CONDITIONAL LOOPING

The looping that we have discussed in the last section is adequate for some applications. However, there are many occasions when we want to be able to modify the conditions of looping *while* the loop is being executed. PASCAL provides some versatile statements that provide just such control.

The UNTIL Construction

One form of loop is provided by the keywords REPEAT and UNTIL. Let us illustrate this.

```
        ⋮
        REPEAT
                     }  PASCAL statements          (4-31)
        UNTIL BOOLEAN statement
        ⋮
```

This program will loop through the PASCAL statements until the BOOLEAN statement becomes TRUE. For instance, consider the program segment

```
BEGIN
   B:=5;
   A:=1;
   D:=Ø;
   REPEAT                                          (4-32)
      A:=A+1;
      C:=B*A;
      D:=D+1;
      E:=2*D
   UNTIL D>2Ø;
```

The statements

```
A:=A+1;
C:=B*A;
D:=D+1;
E:=2*D;
```

will be executed repeatedly until the value of D becomes greater than 2Ø. Note that execution of the loop is terminated by the UNTIL statement so that after D:=D+1 causes the value 21 to be assigned to D, the statement E:=2*D will be executed and *then* the loop will be terminated. A syntax diagram for the UNTIL construction is shown in Fig. 4-3.

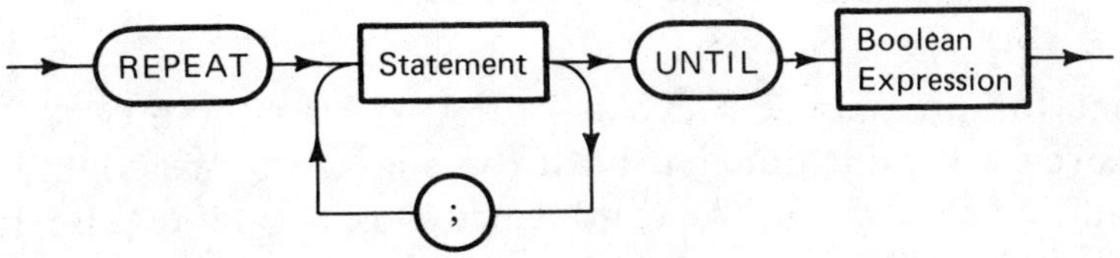

Figure 4-3. Syntax diagram for the REPEAT construction

As another example, let us consider program (4-21) where we calculated the roots of a quadratic equation. Suppose that we have many quadratic equations to solve and that we want the program to repeat until we have solved them all. The person running the program may not know how many equations have to be solved. The REPEAT-UNTIL construction can be used. Each time that an equation must be solved, A, B, and C must be entered. Suppose that, to indicate that we are finished, we input the data A:=1, B:=Ø and C:=Ø. This should terminate execution. A program which accomplishes this is

```
PROGRAM RPTQUADRATICROOTS(INPUT,OUTPUT);
(*REPEATED QUADRATIC ROOT CALCULATION*)
VAR A,B,C,INTVAR,ROOT1,ROOT2:REAL;
BEGIN
  REPEAT
    WRITELN(' ENTER A,B,C');
    READLN(A,B,C);
    INTVAR:=B*B-4.Ø*A*C;
    IF INTVAR>=Ø THEN                                    (4-33)
      BEGIN
        INTVAR:=SQRT(INTVAR);
        ROOT1:=(-B+INTVAR)/(2.Ø*A);
        ROOT2:=(-B-INTVAR)/(2.Ø*A);
        WRITELN(' ROOTS ARE',ROOT1,' AND',ROOT2)
      END
    ELSE
      BEGIN
        INTVAR:=-INTVAR;
        INTVAR:=SQRT(INTVAR)/(2.Ø*A);
        B:=-B/(2.Ø*A);
```

```
            WRITELN(' ROOTS ARE',B,' + OR - I',INTVAR)
        END;
    UNTIL (A=1)AND(B=Ø)AND(C=Ø);
END.
```

Note that the program will cycle with A:=1, B:=Ø and C:=Ø. Thus a final answer will print out that both roots are zero. We could not use the conditions A:=Ø, B:=Ø, C:=Ø since this would require looping through with A:=Ø which would lead to division by Ø and a resulting error.

The WHILE Construction

PASCAL provides another procedure for controlling looping. This construction is similar to the unconditional DO loop discussed in the last section except that the conditions of the DO loop are expressed in terms of a BOOLEAN expression. The general form of this expression is

WHILE(BOOLEAN expression)DO(statement); (4-34)

As long as the BOOLEAN expression is TRUE, the statement will be executed. The statement can be a compound PASCAL expression. The WHILE expression is executed *before* the statement is executed. Thus, once the BOOLEAN expression becomes FALSE, the execution ceases. Note that this contrasts with the UNTIL condition which does not test to see if the controlling BOOLEAN expression is TRUE until after the loop has cycled. A syntax diagram for the WHILE-DO construction is shown in Fig. 4-4.

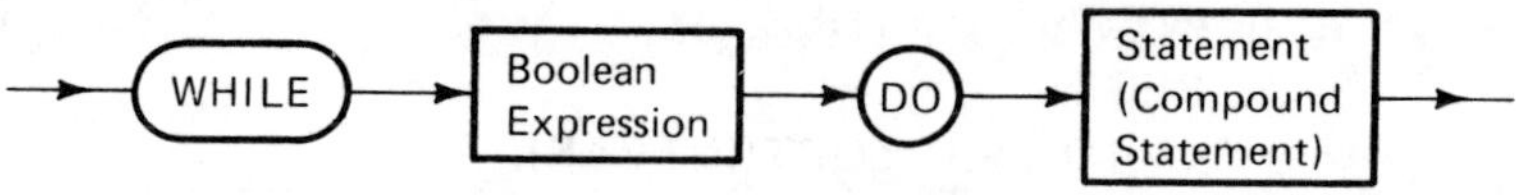

Figure 4-4. Syntax diagram for WHILE-DO looping

As an illustration of this let us modify program (4-33). Now we will have it terminate when A:=Ø, B:=Ø and C:=Ø. Remember that we could not do this before because a "divide by zero" would have resulted.

```
PROGRAM RPTQUADRATICROOTS(INPUT,OUTPUT);
(*REPEATED QUADRATIC ROOT CALCULATION*)
VAR A,B,C,INTVAR,ROOT1,ROOT2:REAL;
```

```
BEGIN
  WRITELN(' ENTER A,B,C');
  READLN(A,B,C);
  WHILE(A<>Ø)OR(B<>Ø)OR(C<>Ø) DO
    BEGIN
      INTVAR:=B*B-4.Ø*A*C;
      IF INTVAR>=Ø THEN
        BEGIN
          INTVAR:=SQRT(INTVAR);                          (4-35)
          ROOT1:=(-B+INTVAR)/(2.Ø*A);
          ROOT2:=(-B-INTVAR)/(2.Ø*A);
          WRITELN(' ROOTS ARE',ROOT1,' AND',ROOT2)
        END
      ELSE
        BEGIN
          INTVAR:=-INTVAR;
          INTVAR:=SQRT(INTVAR)/(2.Ø*A);
          B:=-B/(2.Ø*A);
          WRITELN(' ROOTS ARE',B,' + OR - I',INTVAR)
        END;
      WRITELN(' ENTER A,B,C);
      READLN(A,B,C);
    END;
END.
```

Note that we enter data once before entering the loop and the subsequent data is called for at the end of the loop. The first READLN statement is only executed once. Note that this procedure could not be used with program (4-33) since, if we *initially* entered A:=Ø, B:=Ø, C:=Ø, then the divide by zero condition would result.

Care must be taken when either of the procedures of this section is used. A logical error can cause the looping to persist indefinitely. For instance, the result of the BOOLEAN condition often depends upon calculations within the loop as in program segment (4-32). A logical mistake in the program can cause the looping to continue indefinitely. For instance,

```
B:=-1;
A:=1;
C:=Ø;
REPEAT                                                    (4-36)
```

```
        A:=A+1;
        A:=A*B;
        C:=C+A;
    UNTIL C>20;
    .
    .
    .
```

The value of A that is added to C will always be negative. Hence C will never become greater than 2∅ and the program will remain trapped in the loop indefinitely. Some large computers terminate computation after a fixed time so that not too much valuable computing time is wasted. Nevertheless such conditions should always be avoided.

4-5. NESTED LOOPS

In PASCAL it is possible to nest one loop within another. For instance, in any of the procedures of the last two sections, the compound statements of a loop could contain another loop. In such cases, we say that the inner loop is *nested* within the outer one. As an illustration of this, consider the following program that calculates the Pythagorean triples, that is, the integers that satisfy

$$a^2 + b^2 = c^2 \tag{4-37}$$

The program is to calculate all of the integers that satisfy Eq. (4-37) for a and b between 1 and some entered value of n.

```
PROGRAM PYTHTRIP(INPUT,OUTPUT);
VAR A,B,C,K,M,N:INTEGER;
BEGIN
   WRITELN(' ENTER N');
   READLN(N);
   FOR A:=1 TO N DO (*LOOP 1 STARTS*)
      BEGIN
         FOR B:=A TO N DO (*LOOP 2 STARTS*)
            BEGIN
               K:=A*A+B*B;                                   (4-38)
               C:=B+1;
               REPEAT  (*LOOP 3 STARTS*)
                  M:=C*C;
                  IF M=K THEN WRITELN(A:6,B:10,C:10);
                  C:=C+1;
```

```
            UNTIL M>=K (*LOOP 3 ENDS*)
          END; (*LOOP 2 ENDS*)
      END; (*LOOP 1 ENDS)
  END.
```

Note that comments which are ignored by the compiler can be included to help the programmer keep track of the loops. A value N is entered. There are two loops nested within an outer one. The outer loop is used to vary A between 1 and N. The first nested loop varies B between 1 and N. Thus, all desired values of a and b in Eq. (4-37) are tested. Then K=A*A+B*B is calculated. In the inner REPEAT-UNTIL loop, values of c are tested by comparing K with M:=C*C. If M=K then the corresponding values of A, B and C constitute a Pythagorean triple. Hence, the triple is printed. All values of C starting with J+1 are tried until a triple is found or until M becomes greater than K. At that point the inner loop cycle ends. The procedure is then repeated using the next value of B. After the second loop has cycled completely, the next value of A is used. In this way, all desired values of A and B are used. Note that the smallest value of C is chosen to be equal to B+1 since C must be larger than B. More efficient algorithms for this procedure can be written. This case is just used as an example of the nesting procedure. We shall consider many other examples of nested loops throughout the book.

4-6. THE CASE STATEMENT

The IF-THEN construction discussed earlier allowed the program to have *two* different branches. We shall now consider the CASE statement that allows the program to have many branches. The form of the CASE statement is

```
CASE VARIABLE OF
1:statement a
2:statement b
3:statement c                                    (4-39)
4:statement d
:
END;
:
END.
```

VARIABLE is an INTEGER variable or INTEGER expression whose value is assigned earlier in the program. (Actually, as we shall discuss in Sec. 8-1, VARIABLE need not be of type INTEGER, but it can never be of type REAL.) If VARIABLE:=1, then statement a will be executed and statement b, statement c, . . . will be ignored. Similarly, if VARIABLE:=2, then statement b will be executed and statement a, statement c, . . . will be ignored.

As an example we shall rewrite program (4-22) which calculates quadratic roots. Now we shall consider three different cases, one where the roots are equal ($b^2 - 4ac = \emptyset$), one where there are two different real roots ($b^2 - 4ac > \emptyset$), and the third where the roots have an imaginary component ($b^2 - 4ac < \emptyset$). The program is

```
PROGRAM QUADRATICROOTSCASE(INPUT,OUTPUT);
(*QUADRATIC ROOT CALCULATION*)
VAR A,B,C,INTVAR,ROOT1,ROOT2:REAL;
   CASEVAR:INTEGER;
BEGIN
   WRITELN(' ENTER A,B,C');
   READLN(A,B,C);
   INTVAR:=B*B-4.Ø*A*C;
   IF INTVAR=Ø THEN CASEVAR:=1
      ELSE IF INTVAR>Ø THEN CASEVAR:=2
         ELSE CASEVAR:=3;
   CASE CASEVAR OF
      1:WRITELN(' EQUAL ROOTS',-B/(2.Ø*A);                    (4-4Ø)
      2:BEGIN
         INTVAR:=SQRT(INTVAR);
         ROOT1:=(-B+INTVAR)/(2.Ø*A);
         ROOT2:=(-B-INTVAR)/(2.Ø*A);
         WRITELN(' ROOTS ARE',ROOT1,' AND',ROOT2)
        END;
      3:BEGIN
         INTVAR:=-INTVAR;
         INTVAR:=SQRT(INTVAR)/(2.Ø*A);
         B:=-B/(2.Ø*A);
         WRITELN(' ROOTS ARE',B,' + OR - I',INTVAR)
        END;
   END;
END.
```

There can be considerable variety in numbering the CASE statements. For instance, the following is valid

```
CASE CASEVAR OF
1: statement a
9: statement b
7,8,1Ø: statement c                              (4-41)
3: statement d
END;
:
```

Now if CASEVAR:=1, statement a is executed; if CASEVAR:=9, statement b is executed; if CASEVAR:=7, or if CASEVAR:=1Ø, then statement c is executed; if CASEVAR:=3, then statement d is executed. Note that the constants need not be consecutive. CASEVAR is called the CASE *selector*. A syntax diagram for the CASE construction is shown in Fig. 4-5.

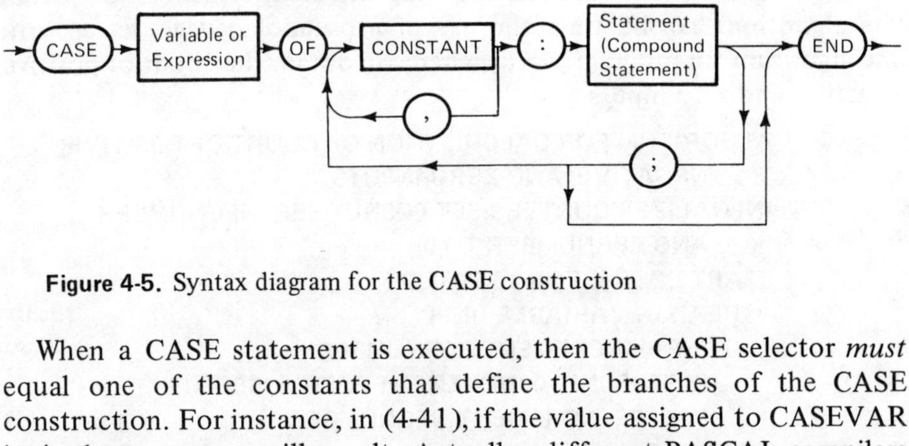

Figure 4-5. Syntax diagram for the CASE construction

When a CASE statement is executed, then the CASE selector *must* equal one of the constants that define the branches of the CASE construction. For instance, in (4-41), if the value assigned to CASEVAR is 4, then an error will result. Actually, different PASCAL compilers will treat this differently so that this situation should be avoided.

4-7. BASIC IDEAS OF STRUCTURED PROGRAMMING

When complex algorithms are written, they often contain logical errors which must be debugged. Special programming techniques have been developed which reduce the number of logical errors that occur and which make debugging or the remaining ones easier. Such programs are called *structured programs*. We shall consider some of the elementary ideas of good programming as well as of structured programming here, and shall discuss additional elements of structured programming in Chapter 7.

Algorithms—Pseudolanguages

The logical ideas implemented by a program constitute an *algorithm*. The algorithm should be conceived before the program is written. There is a great temptation to "jump in" and start programming before completely formulating the algorithm but, in general, except for trivial programs, this is poor practice. The details of the algorithm then get undesirably involved with the syntax of the program.

The algorithm should be written in English (or your native tongue). It is often helpful to write it in a form that resembles the programming language that you are using, in this case, PASCAL. In such cases, the algorithm is said to be written in a *pseudolanguage*. Note that the syntax of the pseudolanguage is *not* formalized so that you do not have to worry about details of syntax during the creative process of writing the algorithm. To illustrate the use of a pseudolanguage, let us write the algorithm for program (4-26) where we obtain the count of positive, negative, and zero inputs.

```
ALGORITHM FOR CALCULATION OF COUNT OF POSITIVE,
      NEGATIVE, AND ZERO INPUTS
INITIALIZE COUNTERS:SET POSNUMBER, NEGNUMBER,
      AND ZERNUMBER TO Ø
START LOOP a (FOR 1Ø TIMES)
   READ IN VARIABLE (INP)                                (4-42)
   IF INP=Ø INCREMENT ZERNUMBER
      ELSE IF INP>Ø INCREMENT POSNUMBER
         ELSE INCREMENT NEGNUMBER
END LOOP a
PRINT COUNTER VALUES
END
```

Note that the use of the pseudolanguage allows us to write an algorithm which, although resembling the final PASCAL program, is free of the details of syntax.

Use of Comments

Once the algorithm is constructed, the program itself has to be written. It is often helpful to include comments within the program to indicate to the programmer or to any other reader what is being done and how it relates to the algorithm. For instance, we could rewrite program (4-26) as

```
PROGRAM POSNEGZERCOUNT(INPUT,OUTPUT);
(*COUNT OF POSITIVE, NEGATIVE AND ZERO VALUES*)
VAR INP:REAL:
  POSNUMBER,NEGNUMBER,ZERNUMBER,COUNT:INTEGER;
BEGIN
(*INITIALIZE COUNTERS*)
  POSNUMBER:=Ø;
  NEGNUMBER:=Ø;
  ZERNUMBER:=Ø;
  FOR COUNT:= 1 TO 1Ø DO (*START LOOPING*)              (4-43)
    BEGIN
      READLN(INP);
      (*TEST FOR POS,NEG OR ZERO*)
      IF INP=Ø THEN ZERNUMBER:=ZERNUMBER+1
        ELSE IF INP>Ø THEN POSNUMBER:=POSNUMBER+1
          ELSE NEGNUMBER:=NEGNUMBER+1;
    END;
  (*OUTPUT RESULTS*)
  WRITELN(' NUMBER OF ZERO INPUTS',ZERNUMBER);
  WRITELN(' NUMBER OF POSITIVE INPUTS',POSNUMBER);
  WRITELN(' NUMBER OF NEGATIVE INPUTS',NEGNUMBER)
END.
```

This is a short program and the comments are relatively simple and, for illustrative purposes, we have used a great many of them. However, too many comments are as bad as too few because they cause program clutter. Obvious comments should be avoided.

Basic Ideas of Program Structure

When complex programs are written, there is usually a great deal of decision making and resultant branching. Let us diagrammatically represent two possible program structures. These diagrams are called *flow charts*. At one time they were widely used to represent algorithms and programs, but most programmers now feel that they are not too useful. However, we can use flow charts to make a point here.

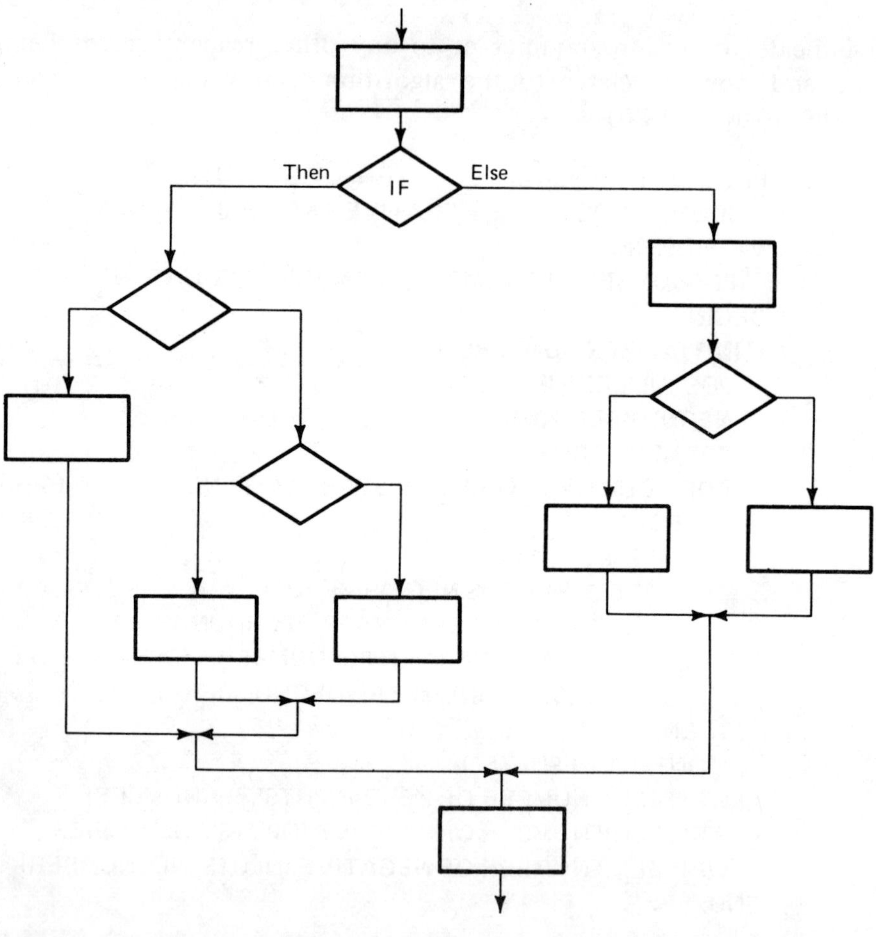

Figure 4-6. Flow chart for a segment of a structured program

In Fig. 4-6 we have a flow chart for a segment which is typical of a good program. The rectangular boxes represent PASCAL statements that do not involve decision making processes, while the diamond-shaped boxes represent decision processes, such as the IF-THEN-ELSE construction. Each diamond-shaped box has two outputs for two possible decisions. Notice how the program of Fig. 4-6 has well defined branches. In general, when programs are written or debugged, each branch can be treated separately and the procedure is simplified. Contrast the diagram with that of Fig. 4-7. Note how the program loops back on itself and how all the branches interact with each other. Although such programs will work, they represent poor programming practice since the program cannot be broken up into simple sections

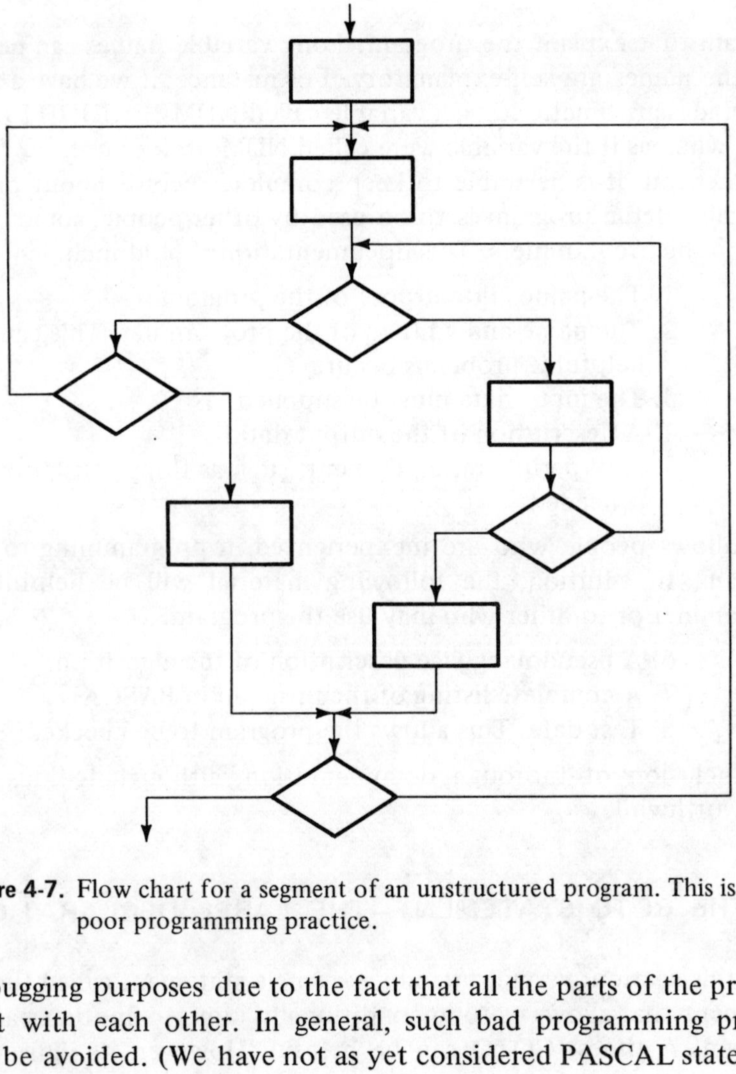

Figure 4-7. Flow chart for a segment of an unstructured program. This is poor programming practice.

for debugging purposes due to the fact that all the parts of the program interact with each other. In general, such bad programming practice should be avoided. (We have not as yet considered PASCAL statements that allow such unstructured back branching.)

Documentation

When you write a program it should be possible for someone else to understand it or, for that matter, for you to understand it if you come back to it after some time has elapsed. Material called *documentation* can be written which describes how the program works, and how to use it. PASCAL has some features that can be used to make the program somewhat self-documenting. We can include comments throughout the program that explain the program. Long variable names can be used so that the names are self-explanatory. For instance, if we have a program that grades arithmetic tests, a variable called NUMBERRIGHT describes itself, whereas if the variable were called NUM, it does not.

In general, it is desirable to keep complete records about programs, especially if the program is to be used by other people, some of whom may not be programmers. This documentation should include:

1. The name and purpose of the program.
2. The name and address of the programmer. This can be very helpful if problems occur.
3. The input data must be supplied.
4. A description of the output data.
5. Any peripheral equipment, such as floppy disk drives, that is needed.

This allows people who are inexperienced in programming to run the program. In addition, the following material will be helpful to the programmer or to other who may use the program:

6. A pseudolanguage description of the algorithm.
7. A complete listing of the program in PASCAL.
8. Test data. This allows the program to be checked.

The inclusion of thorough documentation, although tedious, can be very worthwhile.

4-8. THE GOTO STATEMENT—THE LABEL DECLARATION

In this section we will introduce a single statement called the GOTO statement that allows us to unconditionally jump to another part of the program. A times, GOTO can be helpful. However, its indiscriminate use can lead to the unstructured programs which are prone to logical errors and are difficult to debug, as discussed in Sec. 4-7. Thus, the use of the GOTO statement should usually be avoided. Structured programs are sometimes called "GOTOless" programs. In fact, some compilers which are designed specifically to teach PASCAL to students, do not allow the use of GOTO.

Let us consider the form of the GOTO statement. It is

```
GOTO integer number;
```
(4-44)

The integer must be a number, not a variable, for instance

GOTO 1ØØ; (4-45)

When statement (4-45) is executed, the program will jump to a statement which is numbered 1ØØ. Such numbers are called *labels* and they *must* be declared in a LABEL declaration statement whose form is

LABEL 1ØØ,2ØØ,3ØØ; (4-46)

that is, the word LABEL followed by a list of numbers. With most compilers, the LABEL statement must precede the VAR declaration statement.

The labeled statement is indicated by the label number followed by a colon, for instance,

1ØØ: A:=A+B; (4-47)

A program illustrating these ideas follows.

```
PROGRAM BADFORM(INPUT,OUTPUT);
LABEL 1ØØ,2ØØ,3ØØ;
VAR I,J,K:REAL;
BEGIN                                          (4-48)
   2ØØ:J:=2.5;
   READLN(I);
   IF I<>Ø THEN
      ELSE GOTO 3ØØ;
   1ØØ:J:=J+1;
   IF J<9Ø.4 THEN GOTO 1ØØ
      ELSE K:=J+23.6;
   WRITELN(K);
   GOTO 2ØØ;
   3ØØ:WRITELN(' PROGRAM OVER')
END.
```

In this program, J is assigned the value 2.5 and then I is entered. If the value assigned to I is not Ø, then J is incremented by I. If J<9Ø.4, then the program jumps back to statement 1ØØ and J is again incremented by I. When J>=9Ø.4, then K is computed and printed. The entire program is then repeated and a new value of I is entered. If I=Ø is input, then control moves to statement 3ØØ and the program is ended. Remember that this does not represent good programming form although it *is* proper PASCAL.

Care must be taken if a label is associated with an END. If this is done, then the preceding statement must have a semicolon as its final character.

Note that the statement labels discussed here look like those used for the CASE statements, but they are different. In particular, GOTO statements *cannot reference one of the* "CASE *labels.*" Also note that CASE labels are *not* declared in a LABEL declaration statement.

Although the use of GOTO statements should be avoided, there are times when their use can simplify a program without ruining its structure. In such cases, GOTO statements should be used.

EXERCISES

1. Discuss variables of the type BOOLEAN.
2. If BOOL is a BOOLEAN variable and A, B, C and D are REAL, what will be the value of BOOL after the execution of the following segment?

```
A:=2.3;
B:=4.6;
C:=9.7;
D:=17.8;
BOOL:=A>B;
```

3. Repeat Exercise 2 for

```
BOOL:=A<>D;
```

4. Repeat Exercise 2 for

```
BOOL:=(A>C)OR(A+B=D);
```

5. Repeat Exercise 2 for

```
BOOL:=(A<B)AND(C>D)OR(D>A);
```

6. Repeat Exercise 2 for

```
BOOL:=(A<B)AND((C>D)OR(D>A));
```

7. Describe the operation of the following program segment.

```
  :
D:=4.6;
IF(A+B)>0 THEN D:=2.3;
  :
```

8. Repeat Exercise 7 for

```
        :
D:=4.6;
IF(A+B)>Ø THEN D:=2.3
   ELSE D:=9.Ø;
        :
```

9. Repeat Exercise 7 for

```
        :
D:=4.6;
IF(A+B)>Ø THEN D:=2.3
   ELSE IF A>Ø THEN D:=9.Ø
      ELSE D:=4.3;
        :
```

1Ø. Write a program that inputs three values, which are test grades. It computes their average and then prints "very good" if the average is equal to or greater than 9Ø, "good" if the average is less than 9Ø and equal to or greater than 8Ø, "fair" if the average is less than 8Ø and equal to or greater than 7Ø, poor if the average is less than 7Ø and equal to or greater than 6Ø, and "fail" if the average is less than 6Ø. Check the program by running it on your computer.

11. Write a program that computes the function

$$f(x) = x^2 + 3x + g$$

where x is to be input and

$$g = 2 \text{ if } x<1 \text{ and } g = 5 \text{ if } x\geqslant 1.$$

12. Determine the final value of ITEM after the following program segment is evaluated.

```
        :
ITEM:=3;
FOR I:=1 TO 1Ø DO ITEM:=ITEM+2*I;
        :
```

13. Repeat Exercise 12 for the program segment

```
        :
M:=6;
```

```
N:=4;
ITEM:=3;
FOR I:=N TO M+N DO
   BEGIN
      ITEM:=ITEM+2*I
   END;
   :
```

14. Repeat Exercise 12 for the program segment

```
   :
M:=6;
N:=4;
ITEM:=3;
FOR I=M+N DOWNTO -3 DO
   BEGIN
      ITEM:=ITEM+2*I
   END;
   :
```

15. Repeat Exercise 1Ø but now assume that there are 3Ø students whose grades must be averaged.

16. Write a program to evaluate the function

$$f(x) = x^2 + 3x + 2$$

for integer values of x between 1 and N, where N is a value to be entered by the person running the program. Check the program by running it on your computer.

17. Write a program to evaluate the function

$$f(x,y) = (x+y)^2 + 2x + 3y + 4$$

for x = Ø, Ø.1, Ø.2, . . . , 1.Ø
and y = Ø, Ø.1, . . . , 1.Ø

Check the program by running it on your computer.

18. Determine the final value of ITEM when the following program segment is evaluated

```
   :
ITEM:=Ø;
A:=1;
```

```
B:=2;
REPEAT
   ITEM:=ITEM+A;
   A:=A+B;
UNTIL A>15;
   :
```

19. Repeat Exercise 18 for

```
   :
ITEM:=Ø;
A:=1;
B:=2;
WHILE(A<15)DO
   ITEM:=ITEM+A;
   A:=A+B
END;
   :
```

2Ø. Write a program which evaluates

$$n! = n(n-1)(n-2)\ldots 1$$

where n is an integer. The value of n is to be entered by the user. (Use DO-UNTIL construction.) Check the program by running it on your computer.

21. Repeat Exercise 18 but now use the WHILE-DO construction.

22. Write a program that evaluates

$$1 + \frac{1}{x} + \frac{1}{x^2} + \frac{1}{x^3} + \ldots$$

The value of x is to be entered by the user. The program is to terminate when $|1/x^n| < Ø.ØØØØ1$. The program is not to run if $|x| \leqslant 1$. Check the program by running it on your computer.

23. Write a program that will calculate and print out the values of z and the corresponding values of w, x and y for the function

$$z = x^3 - 2x - y^2 - 3y + w^2 - 1Øw + 25$$

Use values of x between Ø and 1Ø, of y between Ø and 5, and of w between Ø and 6. Steps of Ø.1 should be taken. Also print the maximum and minimum values of z and the corresponding values of x, y and w. Check the program by running it on your computer.

24. Consider the two simultaneous equations

$$y = \sin(x) + \emptyset.1$$
$$y = x$$

They have a solution in the range

$$\emptyset \leqslant x \leqslant \pi$$

Write a program to determine their solution. Check the program by running it on your computer.

25. Write a program that computes f(x) where

$$f(x) = 2x^2 + 3x + 7 \quad \text{if } \emptyset \leqslant x \leqslant 1$$
$$f(x) = 3x^2 - 2x + 9 \quad x < \emptyset$$
$$f(x) = 7x^2 + 9x + 4 \quad x > 1$$

using the CASE statement.

26. What is a pseudolanguage?

27. Write an algorithm in pseudolanguage for the program of Exercise 22.

28. Discuss the ideas of structured programming.

29. What is documentation and why is it important?

3∅. Why is it desirable to avoid GOTO statements?

31. Modify program (4-4∅) using GOTO statements.

Chapter Five

Arrays

We are often called upon to write programs where the same set of calculations must be repetitively performed on a list of variables. In the last chapter we saw that various forms of looping could be used to eliminate the need for rewriting program statements over and over again. In this chapter we shall discuss a procedure which simplifies the manipulation of data used in such programs.

Techniques for using subscripted variables or *arrays* will be presented here. Many mathematical problems are formulated in terms of arrays. In addition, problems involving lists of data also utilize them. For instance, a grading program for 1ØØ students in a class would, in most circumstances, make use of arrays.

5-1. SINGLY SUBSCRIPTED ARRAYS

In mathematics, we often deal with variables that are subscripted. For instance,

$$v_1, v_2, v_3, \ldots$$

The subscripts are used to designate the different variables of type v. In computer programs, all values are printed on a single line. This is because of restrictions that were originally imposed by key punches. Thus, the procedure for writing subscripted variables in PASCAL is

V[1],V[2],V[3],. . .

that is, the subscripts are enclosed within square brackets. Note that not all terminals have square brackets. However, there is some equivalent symbol that can be used. Your computer manual should be checked to ascertain this. The variable can be of any valid PASCAL type. The subscripts *cannot* be REAL. Of the types we have considered, the subscipts must be INTEGER. (We shall consider other data types that can be used in Sec. 8-1.)

The entire set of subscripted variables is called the *array*. The individual terms are called the *elements* of the array. For instance, the VOLTAGE array might consist of the elements

VOLTAGE[1],VOLTAGE[2], and VOLTAGE[3]

Each element of an array is used just like any other PASCAL variable. For instance, the following are valid PASCAL statements

```
A:=VOLTAGE[2]+B;
ITEM:=3;
NUMBER:=2;                                    (5-1)
VOLTAGE[ITEM]:=VOLTAGE[NUMBER*ITEM]+B;
BOX[ITEM]:=VOLTAGE[NUMBER]+BOX[ITEM+3];
```

Each element of the array is treated as a variable. The elements of an array are independent of each other, but they must all be of the same type.

The subscripts of the array can be integers, integer variables, or expressions that yield integers. (Again we shall generalize this to other variable types subsequently.)

When a PASCAL program is written, the variables are defined in the VAR statement. The compiler then reserves storage space for *each* variable, with the amount of storage depending upon the type of variable. REAL variables require more storage space than INTEGERS which, in turn, usually require more storage space than BOOLEAN variables. The array variables must also be declared so that space can be reserved for each element. Since an array can have very many elements, it would be tedious to have to declare all of them. We might have to write 5ØØ or 1ØØØ or more declaration terms. Fortunately, in PASCAL, an array can be declared in a single statement which is part of the VAR declaration. For instance, suppose that we want to declare that the GRADE array has 5ØØ elements which are numbered from 1 to 5ØØ and that the elements of the GRADE array are REAL. We could then write

```
VAR GRADE:ARRAY[1 . . 5ØØ] OF REAL;           (5-2)
```

Note that the form of the declaration is the array name followed by a colon, the word ARRAY followed by square brackets [number 1 . . number 2] containing two integers (not variables) separated by two (and only two) periods. This is then followed by the word OF and then a type specifier. For instance, we could have

```
VAR VOLTAGE:ARRAY[1 . . 100] OF REAL;
    NUMBER:ARRAY[1 . . 500] OF INTEGER;
    TIME:ARRAY[-20 . . 50] OF REAL;                    (5-3)
    A,B,C,D:REAL;
    ITEM,BOX,I,J:INTEGER;
```

Here we have declared VOLTAGE to have 100 REAL elements whose subscripts range between 1 and 100, and TIME to be a REAL array of 71 elements whose subscripts range between −20 and 50. NUMBER has been declared to be an array of 500 INTEGER elements. The numbers 1 . . 100 are called the index specifier. A syntax diagram for this array specification is shown in Fig. 5-1.

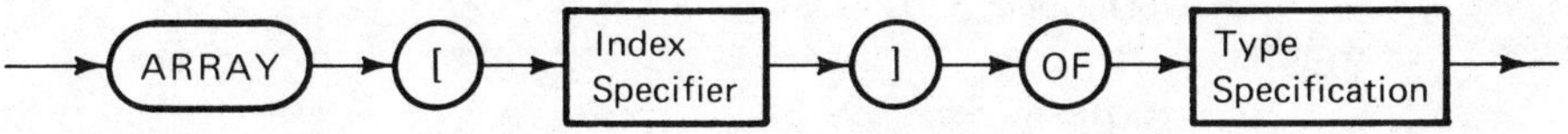

Figure 5-1. Syntax diagram for the specification of a simple one-dimensional array

Let us consider some examples of arrays. Suppose that we want to enter 100 numbers and then obtain their average.

```
PROGRAM AVE100NUMBER(INPUT,OUTPUT);
(*PROGRAM AVERAGES 100 NUMBERS*)
VAR NUMBER:ARRAY[1 . . 100] OF REAL;
      SUM,AVERAGE:REAL;
      COUNT:INTEGER;
BEGIN                                                  (5-4)
   SUM:=0.0;
   FOR COUNT:=1 TO 100 DO
      BEGIN
         READLN(NUMBER[COUNT]);
         SUM:=SUM+NUMBER[COUNT]
      END;
   AVERAGE:=SUM/100.0;
   WRITELN(' AVERAGE=',AVERAGE);
END.
```

The program functions in the following way. Initially, SUM:=0. Now we enter the loop. The first time through the loop, data for NUMBER[1] is read and this value is added to SUM. The second cycle through the loop results in a value's being assigned to NUMBER[2]. This number is then added to SUM. After the complete loop is cycled, the sum of the 1ØØ entries will be obtained, and the average is then computed.

Let us now consider a program which again computes the average. However, now let us assume that we do not know how much data is to be entered, and we will terminate the input by entering a negative number. This is not to be included in the average. We assume that the total number of entries is not to exceed 1ØØ.

```
PROGRAM AVENUMBER(INPUT,OUTPUT);
(*PROGRAM AVERAGES A VARIABLE NUMBER OF NUMBERS*)
VAR NUMBER:ARRAY[1 . . 1Ø1] OF REAL;
    SUM,AVERAGE:REAL;
    COUNT,INDEX:INTEGER;
BEGIN
  COUNT:=Ø;
  (*INPUT DATA*)
  REPEAT
    COUNT:=COUNT+1;                                    (5-5)
    READLN(NUMBER[COUNT]);
  UNTIL NUMBER[COUNT]<Ø.Ø;
  SUM:=Ø.Ø;
  (*OBTAIN SUM*)
  FOR INDEX:=1 TO COUNT-1 DO
    BEGIN
      SUM:=SUM+NUMBER[INDEX]
    END;
  AVERAGE:=SUM/(COUNT-1);
  WRITELN(' AVERAGE=',AVERAGE)
END.
```

We have written the program with two loops, one for entering data and the other for computing the sum. We start by initializing COUNT. Each time that the REPEAT-UNTIL loop is cycled, COUNT is incremented by 1 and a value of the array element NUMBER[COUNT] is assigned. When a negative input is given, the loop is terminated. Now COUNT is one larger than desired and, thus, a negative number, which is not to be included in the average, is stored in the last element of the array. Note that the "compound statement" of the DO loop could be replaced by the statements

```
FOR INDEX:=1 TO COUNT−1 DO
   SUM:=SUM+NUMBER[INDEX];
```

Now consider the DO loop. It loops from INDEX:=1 to COUNT−1. Hence, only the desired elements of the NUMBER array are used to obtain SUM. Note the statement where AVERAGE is obtained. This is actually a mixed mode statement, see Sec. 2-4.

The specification of the size of the array must be done at the beginning of the program which precedes any calculations. We cannot use data to change the size specifications since storage space is reserved when the program is compiled. Thus, in this program, we assume that no more than 1ØØ data elements are to be entered. The last element of the array stores a negative number which is used to terminate input. Thus, we provide that the array has 1Ø1 elements.

As a third example of the use of arrays, let us generalize the averaging idea. Suppose that data is to be punched on data cards. Each card contains a student's ID number and grades in three tests. The program is to print out a table of the students' ID numbers and averages in the three tests. In addition, we want the highest average to be printed. We assume that each card has the grades arranged in the following order

ID NUMBER   GRADE 1   GRADE 2   GRADE 3   (5-6)

It is assumed that there are no more than 299 students.

```
PROGRAM GRADEAVE(INPUT,OUTPUT);
(*PROGRAM AVERAGES STUDENTS' GRADES USING ARRAYS*)
VAR IDNUMBER:ARRAY[1 . . 3ØØ] OF INTEGER;
      GRADE1:ARRAY[1 . . 3ØØ] OF REAL;
      GRADE2:ARRAY[1 . . 3ØØ] OF REAL;
      GRADE3:ARRAY[1 . . 3ØØ] OF REAL;
      AVERAGE:ARRAY[1 . . 3ØØ] OF REAL;
      SUM,MAXAVERAGE:REAL;
      COUNT,ITEM:INTEGER;
BEGIN
   COUNT:=Ø;
   (*OBTAIN DATA*)
   REPEAT
      COUNT:=COUNT+1;
```

```
    READLN(IDNUMBER[COUNT],GRADE1[COUNT],
                GRADE2[COUNT],GRADE3[COUNT])
  UNTIL IDNUMBER[COUNT]=Ø;                      (5-7)
  WRITELN(' ID NUMBER':1Ø,'AVERAGE':8);
  FOR ITEM:=1 TO COUNT-1 DO
    BEGIN
      AVERAGE[ITEM]:=(GRADE1[ITEM]+GRADE2[ITEM]
                    +GRADE3[ITEM])/3.Ø;
      WRITELN(IDNUMBER[ITEM]:1Ø,AVERAGE[ITEM]:8:1)
    END;
  (*OBTAIN MAXIMUM AVERAGE*)
  MAXAVERAGE:=Ø.Ø;
  FOR ITEM:= 1 TO COUNT-1 DO
    BEGIN
      IF AVERAGE[ITEM]>MAXAVERAGE THEN
             MAXAVERAGE:=AVERAGE[ITEM]
    END;
  WRITELN(' MAXIMUM AVERAGE=',MAXAVERAGE)
END.
```

The reading of data is terminated by an input of Ø for the first entry on the data card. The other three entries on that data card are arbitrary, but should be present. The average of each student's grades is then obtained and stored in the AVERAGE array. The student's ID number and average are then printed.

Finally, MAXAVERAGE is set equal to zero and then successively compared with each student's average. If MAXAVERAGE is less than AVERAGE[COUNT], with which it is being compared, then MAXAVERAGE is replaced by the larger value. Thus, when the cycling of the last loop is complete, MAXAVERAGE will equal the maximum average. It might be desirable to modify this procedure so that the averages are printed in descending order, or in order of the ID numbers. We shall discuss procedures for ordering of lists in the next chapter.

5-2. THE TYPE DECLARATION

In the last section we declared each array in a VAR statement. This meant writing the size of the array and other information about it for each array used. Many of the arrays were of the same size and type. In such cases, PASCAL provides a statement which can be helpful. It is the TYPE statement. We have used the concept of a "type" before.

For instance, REAL, INTEGER, and BOOLEAN are types that are defined by the compiler. The TYPE statement allows the programmer to define other specifications as types. As an example of the TYPE statement, the following is equivalent to the declaration part of program (5-7).

```
TYPE BOX=ARRAY[1 . . 3ØØ] OF REAL;
VAR IDNUMBER:ARRAY[1 . . 3ØØ] OF INTEGER;
    GRADE1,GRADE2,GRADE3,AVERAGE:BOX;          (5-8)
    SUM,MAXAVERAGE:REAL;
    COUNT,ITEM:INTEGER;
```

The TYPE statement declares that variables of type BOX are arrays with subscripts ranging from 1 to 3ØØ, containing elements of type REAL. Note that the word BOX is arbitrary. We could have used MATRIX, etc. The form of the TYPE statement is the word TYPE followed by an identifier, an equals sign (no colon), and a specification. In this case we have declared that BOX is a type of variable (e.g. an array). A syntax diagram for the TYPE statement is shown in Fig. 5-2.

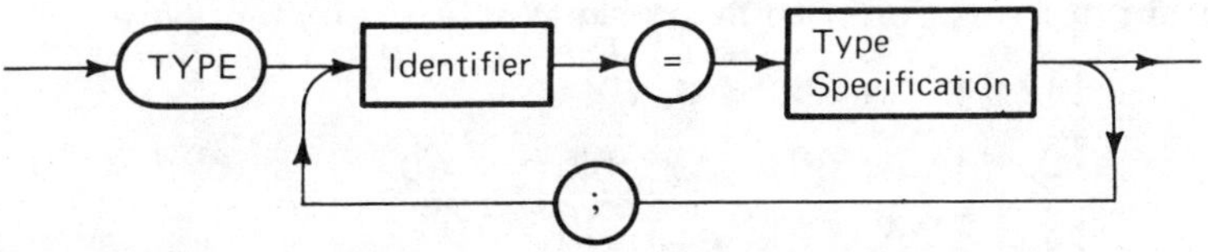

Figure 5-2. Syntax diagram for a TYPE specification

We can make other declarations in the TYPE statement. (Some of these will be discussed in Chapters 6, 8, 9, 1Ø, and 11.) For instance, the following is equivalent to (5-8):

```
TYPE SIZE=1 . . 3ØØ;
    BOX=ARRAY[SIZE] OF REAL;
VAR IDNUMBER:ARRAY[SIZE] OF INTEGER;          (5-9)
    GRADE1,GRADE2,GRADE3,AVERAGE:BOX;
    SUM,MAXAVERAGE:REAL;
    COUNT,ITEM:INTEGER;
```

Again the use of the word SIZE is arbitrary. Here we have declared that the type SIZE represents 1 . . 3ØØ. Then SIZE can be used in place of 1 . . 3ØØ. Now if we wish to change the size of the arrays, we need only change one statement. In subsequent chapters we shall see other versatile uses of the declaration TYPE.

5-3. MULTIDIMENSIONAL ARRAYS

The arrays that we have discussed in the last section could be considered to be long lists of data. As such, they are said to have one dimension. It is sometimes convenient for the programmer to work with tables of data, or arrays, which have rows and columns. Such arrays are said to be two dimensional. Similarly, there are three dimensional and multidimensional arrays. It should be noted that the computer stores all data in long lists, that is, in successive locations in the memory. Thus, the idea of a multidimensional array is somewhat artificial, but it can be of great help to the programmer in organizing programs.

Let us start by considering a simple representation of multidimensional arrays. We shall then extend the concepts. A multidimensional array can be specified by a VAR or TYPE statement. For instance, suppose that we have

```
VAR A:ARRAY[1 . . 3,-1 . . 1]OF REAL;                (5-1Ø)
```

This could be considered to be an array whose elements are

```
A[1,-1]  A[1,Ø]  A[1,1]
A[2,-1]  A[2,Ø]  A[2,1]                              (5-11)
A[3,-1]  A[3,Ø]  A[3,1]
```

To specify a two dimensional array, the size specification is written as two single dimensional size specifiers separated by a comma, that is [integer . . integer,integer . . integer]. TYPE statements can also be used with ARRAY specifications, for instance,

```
TYPE DIM=1 . . 5Ø;
     MATRIX=ARRAY[DIM,DIM] OF REAL;                  (5-12)
VAR GRADE,AVERAGE:MATRIX;
```

Here, GRADE and AVERAGE have both been specified to be two dimensional arrays of 5Ø × 5Ø REAL elements.

As an example of the use of a two dimensional array, let us modify program (5-7). Now, instead of using 5 arrays, we shall use 1 array which has 3ØØ rows and 5 columns. The program is

```
PROGRAM GRADEAVEMULTARRAY(INPUT,OUTPUT);
(*PROGRAM AVERAGES STUDENTS' GRADES USING
     TWO DIMENSIONAL ARRAYS*)
TYPE SIZE=1 . . 3ØØ;
```

```
VAR GRADE:ARRAY[SIZE,1 .. 5] OF REAL;
    SUM,MAXAVERAGE:REAL;
    COUNT,ITEM:INTEGER;
BEGIN
  COUNT:=Ø;
  (*OBTAIN DATA*)
  REPEAT
    COUNT:=COUNT+1;
    READLN(GRADE[COUNT,1],GRADE[COUNT,2],
                GRADE[COUNT,3],GRADE[COUNT,4])
  UNTIL GRADE[COUNT,1]=Ø;                         (5-13)
  WRITELN(' ID NUMBER':1Ø,'AVERAGE':8);
  FOR ITEM:=1 TO COUNT-1 DO
    BEGIN
      GRADE[ITEM,5]:=(GRADE[ITEM,2]+GRADE[ITEM,3]+
                          GRADE[ITEM,4])/3.Ø;
      WRITELN(ROUND(GRADE[ITEM,1]):1Ø,
                         GRADE[ITEM,5]:8:1)
    END;
  (*OBTAIN MAXIMUM AVERAGE*)
  MAXAVERAGE:=Ø.Ø
  FOR ITEM:=1 TO COUNT-1 DO
    BEGIN
      IF GRADE[ITEM,5]>MAXAVERAGE THEN
                         MAXAVERAGE:=GRADE[ITEM,5]
    END;
  WRITELN(' MAXIMUM AVERAGE=',MAXAVERAGE)
END.
```

The first column of the array is used for the ID number. The second, third and fourth columns store the grades. When the average is computed, it will be stored in the fifth column. All of the components of the array must be of the same type. Hence, in this program, the ID numbers are REAL. Since we only want an integer value to be printed for the ID number, we use the ROUND function in conjunction with the WRITELN statement. The other ideas of the program are the same as those of program (5-7). (Note that the last compound statement could be replaced as in the discussion following program (5-5).)

A multidimensional array can be considered to ba an ARRAY whose elements are each an array. For instance, in program (5-13), we could write the array declaration as

```
VAR GRADE:ARRAY[1 . . 3ØØ] OF
                    ARRAY[1 . . 5] OF REAL          (5-14)
```

Now GRADE can be considered to have 3ØØ elements. Each one of these elements is a 5 element array. We can again think of this as an array of 3ØØ rows where each row is composed of 5 elements. Thus, the same ideas that we have discussed before apply here also.

Since a multidimensional array is an array of arrays, there are actually two sets of notation that can be used when the elements of an array are referenced. For instance, the following pairs are equivalent.

```
GRADE[1,3]  and GRADE[1] [3]                  (5-15a)
SAMPLE[25Ø,17]  and  SAMPLE[25Ø] [17]         (5-15b)
```

The first type of notation is useful if the programmer is considering the array to be a two dimensional table, while the second is useful if the programmer is considering that the array has elements which are arrays.

We can also define a three dimensional array. For instance, the following assignment statements could be used.

```
VAR POSITION:ARRAY[1 . . 25,–5 . . 7,
                        Ø . .5Ø] OF REAL;     (5-16a)
```

or

```
VAR POSITION:ARRAY[1 . . 25] OF ARRAY[–5 . . 7]
          OF ARRAY[Ø . . 5Ø] OF REAL;         (5-16b)
```

A syntax diagram for the specification of (5-16a) is given in Fig. 5-3.

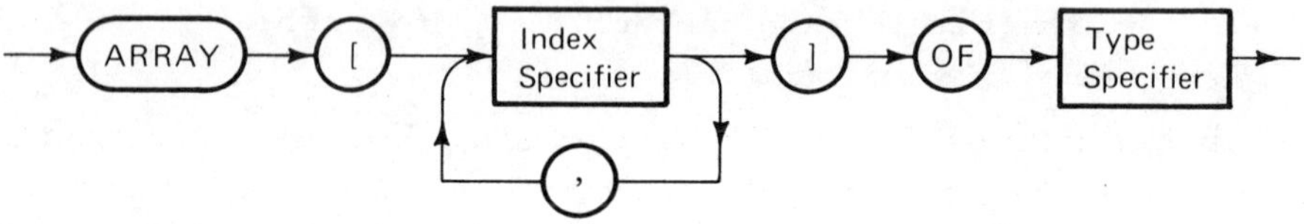

Figure 5-3. Syntax diagram for one form of multidimensional array specification

From specification (5-16), POSITION can then be thought of as a three dimensional array, or as an array each of whose elements is a two dimensional array. The elements of the array could be referenced by either of the following pairs of statements.

```
POSITION[1,–3,6] or POSITION[1] [–3] [6]                (5-17a)
POSITION[I+J,K*B,G] or POSITION[I+J] [K*B] [G]          (5-17b)
```

Note that when INTEGER expressions are used to compute subscripts, the component values must lie within the specifications of the array or an error will result. For instance, in (5-17b), if K*B is less than −5 or greater than 7, an error will result. Most computers will cause execution to cease in such circumstances.

We have illustrated three dimensional arrays. Some PASCAL compilers will allow more dimensions. Your computer manual should be checked to ascertain the maximum number of dimensions allowed.

5-4. ASSIGNMENT AND LOGICAL EXPRESSIONS WITH ARRAYS

Arrays can be set equal to other arrays using simple PASCAL expressions, provided that the size specifications are compatible and that the elements are of the same TYPE. For instance, consider GRADE1 and GRADE2 of program (5-7). We can write

```
GRADE1:=GRADE2;                                              (5-18)
```

This statement sets all of the elements of GRADE1 equal to the corresponding ones of GRADE2. Actually, PASCAL provides more versatile uses of the assignment operation. For instance, suppose that we have the following declaration

```
VAR MATRIX:ARRAY[1 . . 5,1 . . 4,1 . . 3] OF INTEGER;
    RECTANGLE:ARRAY[1 . . 4,1 . . 3] OF INTEGER;             (5-19)
    VECTOR:ARRAY[1 . . 3] OF INTEGER;
```

Then, the following are valid PASCAL statements

```
VECTOR:=RECTANGLE[3];                                        (5-2Ø)
RECTANGLE:=MATRIX[1];                                        (5-21)
```

Let us consider this. RECTANGLE is a [1 . . 4] array, each of whose elements is a [1 . . 3] array, while VECTOR is a [1 . . 3] array. Thus, an element of RECTANGLE has a form that is identical with the VECTOR array. In statement (5-2Ø) we assign one of the elements of RECTANGLE (a [1 . . 3] array) to VECTOR. In a similar way, in statement (5-21), we assign one of the elements of MATRIX to RECTANGLE. Remember that each element of MATRIX is actually a two dimensional array whose specifications are the same as those of RECTANGLE. The following program will provide an example of this.

```
PROGRAM ARRAYEQUALITY(INPUT,OUTPUT);
(*ILLUSTRATION OF SOME ARRAY EQUALITIES*)
```

```
VAR MATRIX:ARRAY[1 . . 5,1 . . 4,1 . . 3] OF INTEGER;
    RECTANGLE:ARRAY[1 . . 4,1 . . 3] OF INTEGER;
    VECTOR:ARRAY[1 . . 3] OF INTEGER;
    I,J,K,L,M,N:INTEGER;
BEGIN
  L:=1;
  FOR I:=1 TO 5 DO
    BEGIN
      FOR J:=1 TO 4 DO
        BEGIN
          FOR K:=1 TO 3 DO
            BEGIN
              MATRIX[I,J,K] :=L;                    (5-22)
              L:=L+1;
            END;
        END;
    END;
  READLN(M);
  RECTANGLE:=MATRIX[M] ;
  I:=1 TO 4 DO
    BEGIN
      FOR J:=1 TO 3 DO
        BEGIN
          WRITELN(RECTANGLE[I,J] :3)
        END;
      WRITELN;
    END;
  READLN(M);
  VECTOR:=RECTANGLE[M] ;
  FOR I:=1 TO 3 DO
    BEGIN
      WRITELN(VECTOR[I] :3)
    END;
  WRITELN
END.
```

If we enter M=1, N=2, then the statement

```
RECTANGLE:=MATRIX[1]
```

results in the following output for RECTANGLE.

1	2	3
4	5	6
7	8	9
1∅	11	12

while the statement

```
VECTOR:=RECTANGLE[2];
```

results in

4 5 6

for VECTOR. Similarly,

```
RECTANGLE:=MATRIX[2];
```

results in the following output for RECTANGLE.

13	14	15
16	17	18
19	2∅	21
22	23	24

We can also write the following valid PASCAL statement.

```
MATRIX[1]:=RECTANGLE                                    (5-23)
```

This results in the value of RECTANGLE's being assigned to the first element of MATRIX. Remember that each element of MATRIX is itself a two dimensional array.

Matrices can be used in conjunction with BOOLEAN expressions using the relational operators = and <>. For instance, using the assignment of (5-19), a valid PASCAL statement is

```
BOOL:=VECTOR=RECTANGLE[3];                              (5-24)
```

Now BOOL will be true if each element of VECTOR is equal to the corresponding element of RECTANGLE[3]. Similarly, if GRADE1 and GRADE2 is each an [1 . . 3∅∅] array of REAL, we can write

```
IF(GRADE1<>GRADE3)THEN A:=3.∅
  ELSE A:=∅.∅;                                          (5-25)
```

Now A will be set equal to 3.∅ unless *each* element of GRADE1 is equal to the corresponding element of GRADE3.

EXERCISES

1. Consider the following program sequence where I and J have been declared INTEGER and A is a one dimensional array.

```
I:=3;
J:=4;
A(I*J):=6.Ø;
A(I–1):=4.Ø;
```

What are the values of A(12) and A(2)?

2. Why must the size of an array be declared at the beginning of a program?

3. Describe the operation of the following program.

```
VAR A:ARRAY[1 .. 1ØØ] OF REAL;
      B:ARRAY[1 .. 1ØØ] OF REAL;
      I:INTEGER;
      ANSWER:REAL;
BEGIN
   FOR I:=1 TO 1ØØ DO A[I] :=2*I;
   FOR I:=2 TO 1ØØ DO B[I–1] :=A[I] *I;
   FOR I:=1 TO 99 DO WRITELN(B[I] );
END.
```

4. Write a PASCAL program that reads in 1ØØ values and stores them in an array and then prints out the largest and smallest values. Check your program by running it on your computer.

5. Modify the program of Exercise 4 so that all the elements of the array are printed in descending order. Check your program by running it on your computer.

6. Modify program (5-5) so that the smallest number is excluded from the average. Check your program by running it on your computer.

7. Modify program (5-7) so that the results are printed out in order of increasing ID number. Check your program by running it on your computer.

8. Write a program using arrays which calculates the function

$$f(x) = a_n x^n + a_{n-1} x^{n-1} + \ldots + a_1 x + a_\emptyset$$

where the coefficients a_n, a_{n-1}, . . . , $a_\emptyset$ are to be entered and stored in an array. The values of x and n are also variables to be entered. Assume that n is less than 2Ø. Check your program by running it on your computer.

9. If you have written the program of Exercise 8 in a straightforward manner, the following program segment for the evaluation of f(x) will provide faster execution.

```
     :
    FOFX:=A(N);
    FOR I:=Ø TO N−1 DO
      BEGIN
        FOFX:=FOFX*X+A(N−1)
      END;
     :
```

   Explain the efficiency of this segment and incorporate it into your program. Check your program by running it on your computer.

1Ø. Discuss the use of the TYPE statement is conjunction with arrays.

11. Explain the following statements

```
    TYPE LENGTH=1 . . 25;
         SIZE=−5 . . 1Ø;
         AREA=ARRAY[LENGTH] OF REAL;
         PLANE=ARRAY[SIZE] OF INTEGER;
    VAR LONG,TRACK,BOX:AREA;
         ITEM,NUMBER:PLANE;
         A,B,C:REAL;
         I;J;K:INTEGER;
```

12. Discuss the meaning of the following statements.

```
    TYPE DEF=ARRAY[1 . . 2Ø,1 . . 3Ø] OF REAL;
    VAR MATRIX,RECT:DEF;
```

13. How many elements does the MATRIX array of Exericise 12 have?

14. Modify program (5-13) so that the arrays are printed in order of increasing ID numbers. Check your program by running it on your computer.

15. Write a program which calculates the function

$$z = an$$

$$z = a_n x^n + a_{n-1} x^{n-1} + \ldots + a_1 x + a_\emptyset$$

$$+ b_m y^m + b_{m-1} y^{m-1} + \ldots + b_1 y + b_\emptyset$$

where the coefficients a_j, b_j and x, y, n and m are to be entered by the user. Assume that n and m are less than 2Ø. Use a multidimensional array. Use the ideas of Exercise 9 here.

16. Write a program that department stores can use to bill customers. Assume that data is supplied on cards. Each data card contains the customer's ID number and the amount of an individual purchase. The total bill for each customer is to be obtained. The cards are not to be read in any particular order. (The cards are not sorted by ID number.) Assume that there are less than 5ØØØ customers and that each one makes no more than 1ØØ purchases. Check your program by running it on your computer.

17. Write a program that stores a one dimensional array equal to part of a two dimensional array using a simple assignment statement. Check your program by running it on your computer.

18. Write a program that sets a one dimensional array equal to part of a three dimensional array using a simple assignment statement. Check your program by running it on your computer.

19. Write a program that inputs two, two dimensional arrays and then determines if every element of one array is equal to the corresponding element of the other. Check your program by running it on your computer.

2Ø. Repeat Exercise 19 but now use three dimensional arrays.

Chapter Six

Characters and Strings

We have thus far only considered the manipulation of numbers, In this chapter, we shall consider manipulation of letters as well as collections of letters which are called *strings*. The individual letters are called *characters*. The programming techniques that we shall discuss here can be used for such things as alphabetizing of lists of names and word processing.

The operations that we shall discuss in this chapter apply to more than just letters. Punctuation marks and numbers can also be treated as characters. Such characters are called *alphanumeric* characters.

6-1. CHARACTER VARIABLES

In PASCAL, we can declare variables to be of type CHAR. This means that they can then represent alphanumeric quantities, including punctuation marks. Variables are declared to be of type CHAR in the following way.

```
VAR LETTER,CHARACTER,NAME:CHAR;
```
(6-1)

Now the words LETTER, CHARACTER and NAME are CHAR variables. We shall discuss manipulations with CHAR variables in subsequent sections of this chapter. Now let us consider the input and output of data and assignment of values.

Actually, the output of data is essentially the same as that for the output of numeric variables that we discussed in Chapter 3. However, when data is input, special care must be taken. When we work with only INTEGER and/or REAL variables, then a blank space can be used as a delimiter. However, when we use CHAR variables, then a blank space will be interpreted as a character. This can prove troublesome. Consider the program segment

```
VAR C:CHAR;
     A,B:INTEGER;                    (6-2)
BEGIN
   READLN(A,C,B);
```

Now let us suppose that data is entered on a card using blanks as delimiters as

2∅bAb3

An error will result. The number 2∅ will be assigned to A as desired, but now the blank will be interpreted as a CHAR variable and will be assigned to C. Now B must be read, but the character A, not a number, is the next data on the card. Thus an error will result. If we entered

2∅Ab3

then we would assign A:=2∅; C:=A; B:=3;. The rule is that when a CHAR variable is read, a blank is interpreted as any other character. Thus, if a CHAR variable is called for, and the blank is the next data on the card, then the blank will be assigned to the CHAR variable. On the other hand, if the next value to be read is a REAL or an INTEGER, then the blank will still be interpreted as a delimiter.

Even stranger results can occur. For instance, suppose that we have

```
VAR C1,C2,C3,C4:CHAR;
     A,B,C:INTEGER;
BEGIN                                (6-3)
   READ(A,C1,C2);
   READ(C3,C4);
```

Now suppose that the data cards appear as

26RQ
CD

The blanks after Q on the first card would be interpreted as characters and, hence, the value assigned to C3 and to C4 would be that for a blank. If we replace the READ statements of (6-3) by

```
READ(A,C1,C2);
READLN;                              (6-4a)
READ(C3,C4);
```

or by

```
READLN(A,C1,C2);                                          (6-4b)
READ(C3,C4);
```

then, after C2 is read, a new card would be required. Hence, the assignment would be

```
A:=26;
C1:='R';
C2:='Q';                                                  (6-5)
C3:='C';
C4:='D';
```

Complications can result if numbers are to be input as characters when using READ statements which also contain REAL or INTEGER quantities. For instance, consider the program segment

```
VAR C1:CHAR;
      A,B:INTEGER;                                        (6-6)
BEGIN
   READ(A,B,C1);
```

There is no way that a numerical value can be input for C1. For instance, if the data is

23b15b6

then we have the assignments

```
A:=23;
B:=51;                                                    (6-7)
C1:=' ';
```

If the blank after the 5 is omitted, then 516 would be assigned to B.

Most of the problems that result when CHAR variables are read can be avoided if we do not intermix the reading of CHAR and REAL or INTEGER variables, or if we read them in the proper order. For instance, the problem associated with program sequence (6-6) can be simply resolved if the READ statement is replaced by

```
READ(C1,A,B);                                             (6-8)
```

Now the first item of data will be assigned to C1 and the previously discussed problem will not arise.

We have discussed entering of data using data cards. Similar ideas prevail if the input is from a terminal. There may be some differences. For instance, consider program sequence (6-6). Suppose that the line of data entered is

51 23R

After R is entered, the computation may proceed without any further action on the part of the user. That is, the return may not have to be pressed. Input may vary from computer to computer, but the ideas expressed in this section should be considered in order to avoid problems.

Assignment of Values to CHAR Variables Within the Program

If we want to assign a value to a character variable during the execution, we do it in a manner similar to that for REAL and INTEGER variables. For instance, if C1 and C2 are CHAR variables, then the following are valid PASCAL statements

```
C1:='A';                                    (6-9)
C2:='5';
```

The character value A would be assigned to C1 and the character value 5 would be assigned to C2. Note that when characters are assigned during the body of a program, they *must* be enclosed within single quotes (i.e. the apostrophe), but when data is entered from a terminal or from data cards, quotes *are not* used. In particular, if quotes are used on input, they will be interpreted as characters themselves. For instance, if a character is called for and 'G' is entered, then the character value assigned will be ', and not G.

6-2. OPERATIONS WITH CHAR VARIABLES

We can apply many of the operations that have already been discussed to CHAR variables. Note however that the arithmetic operations of addition, subtraction, multiplication and division cannot be applied to CHAR variables.

In the last section we noted that the usual PASCAL assignement (:=) can be applied to character variables. The BOOLEAN operations can also be applied to character variables. For instance, if BOOL is a BOOLEAN variable and CHAR1 and CHAR2 are character variables, then the following are valid PASCAL statements:

```
BOOL:=CHAR1=CHAR2;                          (6-1Ø)
BOOL:=CHAR1<>CHAR2;                         (6-11)
```

In (6-1∅) BOOL will be TRUE if CHAR1 and CHAR2 are the same and BOOL will be FALSE if CHAR1 and CHAR2 are different. The converse applies for expression (6-11). We can use the BOOLEAN expressions in conjunction with the other operators that we have discussed. For instance,

```
WHILE CHAR1>CHAR2 DO
   BEGIN
   .
   .                                    (6-12)
   .
   END;
```

or

```
IF CHAR1<CHAR3 THEN A:=B+1              (6-13)
   ELSE A:=∅;
```

It may seem strange that the inequality relational operators can be used with characters. However, each character has an integer number, called its *ordinal number*, associated with it. When two characters are compared in a BOOLEAN expression, it is actually their ordinal numbers that are compared.

There are PASCAL functions that enable us to determine and use these ordinal numbers. They are

```
ORD(CH)                                 (6-14)
```

and

```
CHR(INT)                                (6-15)
```

ORD(CH) returns an integer whose value is the ordinal number for the character assigned to CH. The function CHR returns a CHAR variable which is represented by the ordinal number INT. For instance, the following sequence of statements will result in the printing of the ordinal numbers that represents the input character.

```
VAR C:CHAR;
BEGIN
   READLN(C);                           (6-16)
   WRITELN(ORD(C))
END.
```

Two other functions that were introduced in Chapter 2 can be applied to character variables. These are SUCC and PRED. For instance, if we write

```
CHAR1:='2';
CHAR2:=SUCC(CHAR1);
```
(6-17)

then the value assigned to CHAR2 is the character whose ordinal number is one more than that of the character '2.' In general, this will be the character '3.'

We can combine both expressions of (6-17) as

```
CHAR2:=SUCC('2');
```
(6-18)

The ordinal numbers are not standard from one PASCAL system to another. However, there are some characteristics which are. The ordinal numbers which represent letters are such that

```
ORD('A')<ORD('B')<ORD('C')<..<ORD('Z')
```
(6-19)

Note that this does not say that ORD('B') is exactly one greater than ORD('A'), although in some systems it may be. Also note that there are two sets of alphabetical characters, one representing the upper case letters and the other representing the lower case letters. In some commonly used systems, the ordinal numbers of all the lower case letters are greater than those for the upper case letters.

Now let us consider the digits as characters. In general,

```
ORD('Ø')<ORD('1')<..<ORD('9')
```
(6-2Ø)

However, we can make a stronger statement for numbers.

```
SUCC('Ø')='1'
SUCC('1')='2'
  .
  .
  .
SUCC('8')='9'
```
(6-21)

The implication of Eqs. (6-21) is that while ORD('Ø') will not actually be Ø, ORD('8')–ORD('Ø') will return an integer value of 8, ORD('7')–ORD('4') will return an integer value of 3, etc.

As an example of the use of characters, let us consider the following program. We want to enter a radius and compute either the volume of a sphere whose radius is the entered one, or the area of a circle with the given radius, or the circumference of the circle with the given radius. The letter V, C or A will also be input to indicate whether the volume, circumference or area, respectively, is to be calculated.

```
PROGRAM ROUND(INPUT,OUTPUT);
(*USE OF CHARACTERS WITH CASE STATEMENT*)
CONST PI=3.1415926;
VAR AREA,CIRCUMFERENCE,VOLUME,RADIUS:REAL;
    CH:CHAR;
BEGIN
  READLN(RADIUS);
  READLN(CH);
  CASE CH OF
       'V':BEGIN                                        (6-22)
             VOLUME:=4.Ø*PI*RADIUS*RADIUS*RADIUS/3.Ø;
             WRITELN(' VOLUME=',VOLUME)
           END;
       'A':BEGIN
             AREA:=PI*RADIUS*RADIUS;
             WRITELN(' AREA=',AREA)
           END;
       'C':BEGIN
             CIRCUMFERENCE:=2.Ø*PI*RADIUS;
             WRITELN(' CIRCUMFERENCE=',CIRCUMFERENCE)
           END;
  END;
END.
```

Thus we see that CHAR variables can be used to indicate the branching of a CASE block, and also can be used in all of the branching instructions that we have considered.

6-3. STRINGS OF CHARACTERS

Let us now consider how PASCAL program which manipulate strings of characters can be written. Since all text material can be considered to be character strings, string manipulating programs can be used for such things as alphabetizing and word processing.

Strings are made up of individual characters so that a useful procedure would be to store the string in an array (each element of the array is one character). For instance, suppose that we have a string that will have no more than 3Ø characters. We can write

```
VAR WORDS:PACKED ARRAY[1 .. 3Ø] OF CHAR;
  .
  .
  .
  FOR I:=1 TO 3Ø DO                                    (6-23)
    BEGIN
      READ(WORDS(I))
    END;
```

Note the word PACKED. We shall explain it in the next section. For the time begin, assume that all strings are stored in PACKED ARRAYS. Not all PASCAL compilers will allow the use of the READ statement in conjunction with a PACKED ARRAY. In programs (6-31) and (6-34) and in Sec. 6-4 we shall discuss how this problem can be overcome. Now, if the data

THE QUICK BROWN FOX (6-24)

is entered on a line of the terminal, it will be stored in the packed array called WORDS. Note that there are 19 characters (including blanks) in (6-24). Thus, the remaining blanks (11) on the data card will be interpreted as data and stored in the WORDS array. If data is entered from a terminal, then the 11 blanks will have to be physically entered. We shall see how this can be overcome later in this section.

We can also use strings in assignment statements within the body of the program. Now quotes must be used. For instance,

```
STRINGS:='THE QUICK BROWN FOX';                        (6-25)
```

Note that the name of the ARRAY, with no subscripts, is used to the left of the assignment sign.

Suppose that we have two character arrays, which are one dimensional and equal in length, called STRINGS1 and STRINGS2. Then, the following is a valid PASCAL statement

```
STRINGS2:=STRINGS1;                                    (6-26)
```

This causes each element of STRINGS2 to be assigned the value of the corresponding element of STRINGS1. If STRINGS1 and STRINGS2 are not of the same size, then this equality cannot be used. In general, the rules for assignment of arrays as given in Sec. 5-3 apply to character arrays. Note that we can assign individual elements of an array to another array even if they are not of the same size. For instance,

```
VAR WORDS:PACKED ARRAY[1 .. 3Ø] OF CHAR;
    LISTS:PACKED ARRAY[1 .. 1Ø] OF CHAR;
```

```
        .
        .
        .
FOR I:=1 TO 10 DO                                  (6-27)
   BEGIN
      LISTS[I]:=WORDS[I]
   END;
        .
        .
        .
```

Two strings of *equal length* can be compared using the usual BOOLEAN expressions. For instance, if we have

```
STRINGS1:='ABCDEF';                                (6-28)
WORDS:='ABCDEG';
```

then

```
BOOL:=WORDS>STRINGS1;                              (6-29)
```

will be TRUE since ORD(G)>ORD(F). When strings are compared, their numerical values are compared letter by letter. For instance, in the previous case, if

```
ORD(WORDS[1])>ORD(STRINGS1[1])
```

then

```
WORDS>STRINGS1
```

If

```
WORDS[1]=STRINGS1[1]
```

then the second characters are compared. If the second characters are equal, then the third characters are compared, etc. If we had not used PACKED ARRAYS, then many PASCAL compilers would not allow these BOOLEAN comparisons.

We can compare a variable with a constant. For instance, if

```
VAR WORDS:ARRAY[1 . . 5] OF CHAR;
        .
        .
        .
IF WORDS='SMITH' THEN WRITELN(' SMITH PRESENT)      (6-30)
   ELSE WRITELN(' SMITH ABSENT');
```

As an example of some string manipulations, let us write a program that alphabetizes a list of names. We shall assume that each name is no more than 15 characters long.

```
PROGRAM ALPHABETIZE(INPUT,OUTPUT);
```

```
(*PROGRAM ALPHABETIZES A LIST OF NAMES*)
VAR NAMES:PACKED ARRAY[1 .. 5Ø,1 .. 15] OF CHAR;
     SUM:PACKED ARRAY[1 .. 15] OF CHAR;
     CH1:CHAR;
     I,J,K,MARKER:INTEGER;
BEGIN                                                        (6-31)
   (*INPUT DATA*)
   I:=Ø;
   REPEAT
      I:=I+1;
      FOR J:=1 TO 15 DO (*NAME READING LOOP*)
         BEGIN
            READ(CH1);
            NAMES[I,J] :=CH1
         END;
      READLN;
   UNTIL(NAMES[I] ='               '); (*15 BLANK SPACES*)
   FOR J:=1 TO I-1 DO (*OUTER ALPHABETIZING LOOP*)
      BEGIN
         SUB:='ZZZZZZZZZZZZZZZ'; (*15 Z*)
         FOR K:=1 TO I-1 DO (*INNER ALPHABETIZING LOOP*)
            BEGIN
               IF SUB>NAMES[K] THEN
                  BEGIN
                     SUB=NAMES[K] ;
                     MARKER:=K
                  END;
            END;
         WRITELN(NAMES[MARKER] );
         NAMES[MARKER] :='ZZZZZZZZZZZZZZZ'
      END; (*END OF OUTER LOOP*)
END.
```

Note that a two dimensional array is used to store the names. Each row stores one name. Each name is read in the NAME READING LOOP. Actually, each character is read into the variable CH1. This is then assigned to NAMES[I,J] . On some compilers this is necessary because of the use of the packed array. That is, we cannot have READLN (NAMES [I,J]). On other compilers this is permissible. We shall discuss packed arrays in the next section. The READLN following the loop causes the next data to be read from a new card or new line. When a blank card or line is entered, the procedure is terminated.

We start by storing a string SUB which is equal to 15 Z's. This string will be larger in equivalent numerical value than any of the names. Now we compare SUB with the first name. If the character assigned to SUB is treater than that assigned to NAMES[1], then the character assigned to SUB becomes NAMES[1]. After the inner loop has cycled completely, SUB will be assigned the name that is alphabetically first, and K will be assigned the integer that is equal to its row in the NAMES array. Now NAMES[K] is set equal to 'ZZZZZZZZZZZZZZZ'. Thus, NAMES[K] now becomes alphabetically at the end of the list. The outer loop then cycles again. Now the second name on the list is printed. After the cycling of the outer loop is complete, the entire alphabetized list will be printed.

The TYPE statement can also be used with the specifications of character arrays. For instance,

```
TYPE ABC=PACKED ARRAY[1 . . 1ØØ] OF CHAR;
     WORDS=ARRAY[1 . . 1ØØØ] OF ABC;                    (6-32)
VAR NAMES,ADDRESSES:WORDS;
```

Now NAMES and ADDRESSES will each be an array with 1ØØØ elements, where each element consists of a packed array of 1ØØ CHAR variables. The use of ABC in (6-32) is arbitrary, and merely illustrates that any valid identifier can be used here. A better choice would be a more descriptive name such as STRINGS.

If program (6-31) is run from a terminal, then 15 symbols must be entered for each line. If a name that is shorter than 15 characters is to be entered, then additional blanks must be input at its end. This makes the entering of data tedious. In PASCAL there is a BOOLEAN function called EOLN which is a great help in these cases. When data is entered EOLN is FALSE until the return symbol. It then become TRUE. Now we can input variable length strings. For instance, consider program (6-33) which is a modification of program (6-31).

```
PROGRAM ALPHABETIZE(INPUT,OUTPUT);
(*PROGRAM ALPHABETIZES A LIST OF NAMES*)
TYPE STRINGS=PACKED ARRAY[1 . . 15] OF CHAR;
VAR NAMES:ARRAY[1 . . 5Ø] OF STRINGS;
     SUB:STRINGS;
     CH1:CHAR;
     I,J,K,MARKER:INTEGER;
BEGIN
```

```
(*INITIALIZE ARRAYS*)
FOR I:=1 TO 15 DO SUB[I]:=' ';
FOR I:=1 TO 5Ø DO NAMES[I]:=SUB;
(*INPUT DATA*)
I:=Ø;
REPEAT
   I:=I+1;
   J:=Ø;
   REPEAT
      J:=J+1;
      READ(CH1);                                          (6-33)
      NAMES[I,J]:=CH1;
   UNTIL EOLN;
   READLN;
UNTIL(NAMES[I,1]=' ');
FOR J:=1 TO I-1 DO (*OUTER ALPHABETIZING LOOP*)
   BEGIN
      SUB:='ZZZZZZZZZZZZZZZ'; (*15 Z*)
      FOR K:=1 TO I-1 DO (*INNER ALPHABETIZING LOOP*)
         BEGIN
            IF SUB>NAMES[K] THEN
               BEGIN
                  SUB:=NAMES[K];
                  MARKER:=K
               END;
         END; (*END OF INNER LOOP*)
      WRITELN(NAMES[MARKER]);
      NAMES[MARKER]:='ZZZZZZZZZZZZZZZ'
   END; (*END OF OUTER LOOP*)
END.
```

The REPEAT-UNTIL construction is used now to read in the data. When EOLN becomes TURE, the loop terminates. Now that when EOLN is used with noncharacter variables, the operation may not be exactly as described. Your computer manual should be checked to determine the behavior of EOLN under those circumstances.

When comparisons and assignments are performed, we *must* work with strings of equal length. The data is all stored in 15 character strings. At the start of the program, each character of each of the strings is set equal to a blank. If a name of less than 15 characters is input, the remainder of "its" string remains blank. Note that we have also modified program (6-33) to use TYPE declarations.

We have seen that some compilers do not allow the use of statements such as READLN(NAMES[MARKER] where NAMES is a PACKED ARRAY OF CHAR. Some of these compilers do allow the use of another data type called STRING. Variables of TYPE STRING are essentially PACKED ARRAYS OF CHAR but can be used with both input and output statements as well as with assignments and all of the BOOLEAN comparisons discussed earlier. For instance, the following program is a modification of (6-33) using variables of TYPE STRING. Note that the number in the square brackets specifies the length of the string (3∅ in this case).

```
PROGRAM ALPHABETIZE(INPUT,OUTPUT);
(*PROGRAM ALPHABETIZES A LIST OF NAMES*)
VAR NAMES:ARRAY[1 .. 5∅] OF STRING[3∅] ;
    SUB:STRING[3∅] ;
    CH1:CHAR;
    I,J,K,MARKER:INTEGER;
BEGIN                                                  (6-34)
  I:=∅;
  REPEAT
    I:=I+1;
    READLN(NAMES[I] );
  UNTIL NAMES[I]=' ';
  FOR J:=1 TO I-1 DO (*OUTER ALPHABETIZING LOOP*)
    BEGIN
      SUB:='ZZZZZZZZZZZZZZZZZZZZZZZZZZZZZZ'; (*30 Z*)
      FOR K:=1 TO I-1 DO (*INNER ALPHABETIZING LOOP*)
        BEGIN
          IF SUB>NAMES[K] THEN
            BEGIN
              SUB:=NAMES[K] ;
              MARKER:=K
            END;
        END; (*END OF INNER LOOP*)
      WRITELN(NAMES[MARKER] );
      NAMES[MARKER] :='ZZZZZZZZZZZZZZZZZZZZZZZZZZZZZZ'
    END; (*END OF OUTER LOOP*)
END.
```

We can input any length string up to 3∅ characters. The input of a string will be terminated by a line feed. Note that this is convenient in that we do not have to write statements involving EOLN. The size of the strings with which we can work is limited. Typically, the maximum length is 256 characters.

There is a STRING library FUNCTION that is often helpful. It is called CONCAT. For instance, consider the following program.

```
PROGRAM STRCONCAT(INPUT,OUTPUT);
(*ILLUSTRATION OF CONCATENATION OF STRINGS*)
VAR INP1,INP2:STRING[5] ;
     OUT1:STRING[1Ø] ;
BEGIN                                              (6-35)
   READLN(INP1);
   READLN(INP2);
   OUT1:=CONCAT(INP1,INP2);
  WRITELN(OUT1)
END.
```

OUT1 will be a string which is constructed by appending INP2 to the end of INP1. More than two strings can be used in CONCAT. String constants can also be written, for instance,

```
OUT1:=CONCAT(INP1,' ABC',INP2);
```

Now OUT1 will be a string which is composed of the string assigned to INP1, followed by ABC, followed by the string assigned to INP2. There are other STRING FUNCTIONS. These are listed in Appendix B.

6-4. THE PACKED ARRAY

In Sec. 6-3 we designated those arrays used for strings as PACKED ARRAYs. Some PASCAL compilers require the use of the PACKED ARRAY for certain character manipulations such as BOOLEAN comparisons. On the other hand, some operations are not allowed with PACKED ARRAYs. Your computer manual should be checked to ascertain this. In this section we shall describe what is meant by packing an array and also some PACKED ARRAY manipulations.

Computer memories are arranged into groups of bits (i.e. binary digits) called *words*. When REAL or INTEGER variables are stored, the utilization of the memory is very efficient since the amount of storage for each of these types of variable is an integral number of words. For instance, suppose that it takes two words to store each INTEGER. If we have an array of 1ØØ elements, then 2ØØ words will be required to store this array, and every bit will be used with no wasted space. When strings are stored, this may not be the case. For instance, suppose that four bits are required to store a word and that the computer uses 16 bit words. Using the usual storage procedures, each character will be stored in a new word. Hence, each character will "use up" 16 bits, rather than the 4 that are really needed. This is wasteful of space. For instance, in the previous example, if we wanted to store 1ØØ characters, 1ØØ memory words would be required. On the other hand, if we could store more than one character in a single memory word, we might store 4 characters in each memory word and only 25 memory words would be needed. When programs contain a great deal of data, there may not be enough memory available. Thus, it would be desirable not to "waste" memory.

In PASCAL the use of the PACKED ARRAY declaration causes the compiler to conserve memory by storing as much data as possible in a single memory word. For instance, in the previous example, it would cause four CHAR variables to be stored in each memory word. That is,

```
VAR WORDS:ARRAY[1 .. 1ØØ] OF CHAR;
```

would be the ordinary declaration, while if we conserve storage space, we would write

```
VAR WORDS:PACKED ARRAY[1 .. 1ØØ] OF CHAR:
```

We could store INTEGER and REAL data in PACKED ARRAYs. However, as we discussed earlier, this is usually not done since there is no need to conserve space when these kinds of variables are stored.

When certain CHAR operations are performed, with some compilers, the use of the PACKED ARRAY is required. For instance, operations such as the relational ones of $<$ and $>$ can only be performed using packed arrays. Thus, it might seem as though we should always use packed arrays. However, operations with packed arrays are often slower than those with unpacked ones and, as we have seen in the last section, some operations cannot be performed with packed arrays.

We can unpack an array, that is, we can take the data stored in it and assign the values to an unpacked array. This array can then be used for all ordinary array manipulation. The procedure of unpacking may seem to be wasteful of storage space, but there are occasions when it is used. It will certainly be used if it is more convenient to use a packed array in one part of the program and an unpacked array in another part. In addition, there are occasions when many PACKED ARRAYs are stored in a program but, at any one time, we work with only one of them. We can read the data in the PACKED ARRAY in question into the unpacked one, perform the operations with the unpacked array, and then read the data back into the PACKED ARRAY. Let us illustrate this. Suppose that we have

```
TYPE STRINGS=PACKED ARRAY[1 . . 1ØØØ] OF CHAR;
VAR WORDS,NAMES,GRADES,PEOPLE:STRINGS;              (6-36)
      BUFFER:ARRAY[1 . . 1ØØØ] OF CHAR;
```

Suppose that we want to unpack WORDS, read it into BUFFER, perform some operation, and then return the information to WORDS. We could do the following

```
(*LOAD WORDS INTO BUFFER*)
FOR I:=1 TO 1ØØØ DO BUFFER[I] :=WORDS[I] ;
  .
  .                   } calculations using BUFFER
  .
(*RETURN DATA TO WORDS*)
FOR I:=1 TO 1ØØØ DO WORDS[I] :=BUFFER[I] ;
```

(The last step, where data is returned to WORDS, is unnecessary, unless the calculations changed BUFFER.) The same procedure could be repeated with the other packed arrays.

Actually, if there are several packed arrays with different size specifications, then the array used for unpacking must be larger than any of them. For instance, we may have

```
VAR WORDS:PACKED ARRAY[M . . N] OF CHAR;            (6-37)
      BUFFER:ARRAY[K . . J] OF CHAR;
```

where K, J, M, and N are integer constants and

$$J - K \geqslant N - M \tag{6-38}$$

Now a typical unpacking operation would be

```
FOR INDEX:=M TO N DO BUFFER[INDEX-M+I] :=
                      WORDS[INDEX] ;                (6-39)
```

Some PASCAL compilers provide a single instruction that performs the operation of (6-39). It is usually more efficient than the use of the DO loop. The instruction is

```
UNPACK(WORDS,BUFFER,I);                             (6-4Ø)
```

Executing either (6-39) or (6-4Ø) causes the values in WORDS to be read into the first J−I locations of BUFFER.

The packing operation can be described by

```
FOR INDEX:=M TO N DO WORDS[INDEX] :=
                     BUFFER[INDEX−M+I];          (6-41)
```

The corresponding single instruction is

```
PACK(BUFFER,I,WORDS);                            (6-42)
```

INDEX should be a variable that is not used elsewhere in the program.

EXERCISES

1. What is meant by character data?
2. Discuss the following sequence of statements and the problems that can arise when data is entered.

```
VAR CH1,CH2,CH3:CHAR;
    I,J,K,L:INTEGER;
BEGIN
  READ(CH1,I,CH2,J,CH3);
```

3. Using the assignments of Exercise 2, discuss the following statements.

```
CH2:='I';
J:=I;
```

4. Write a program that enables you to determine the ordinal numbers for all the characters that you can input. Determine these ordinal numbers for your computer.
5. What is meant by a string?
6. When are single quotes used in conjunction with string data?
7. Discuss the following statements

```
TYPE STRING=PACKED ARRAY[1 . . 1ØØ] OF CHAR;
VAR WORDS:STRING;
    PAGES:ARRAY[1 . . 5Ø]OF STRING;
```

8. Write a program that inputs a list of words and then prints all those whose first character is an A. Check the program by running it on your computer.
9. Repeat Exercise 8 but now print all the words whose second character is an E.

10. Write a program that inputs a list of names and indicates how many of those are SMITH. Check your program by running it on your computer.
11. Modify program (5-13) so that the students' names can be printed out with the other data.
12. Repeat Exercise 11 but now have the data printed in alphabetical order.
13. Modify the program of Exercise 5-16 so that the customer's name is also printed out.
14. Modify the program of Exercise 10 using the EOLN.
15. Discuss the meaning of packed and unpacked arrays.
16. Write a program that unpacks and then packs an array. Check the program by running it on your computer.

Chapter Seven

Subprograms—Further Discussion of Structured Programming

We shall now discuss techniques which can be used to greatly simplify some programs. In addition, these techniques can be of great help in writing structured programs.

There are times when the same type of calculation is repeated at many points thoughout a program. For instance, we might take the cube root of a number several times in the program. We could, of course, repeat the program statements wherever they were needed, but subprograms which can be called by the main program can be used to save time and space. For examples, the library functions that we discussed in Chapter 2 are such subprograms. If we want to take the square root, we do not have to write a sequence of program steps, but need merely to use SQRT. In a similar way, the programmer can write his own PASCAL subprograms. These are of two types, the PROCEDURE and the FUNCTION. We shall discuss both of them in this chapter.

The use of procedures and function often allow us to break up a complex program into a set of simpler subprograms, which naturally leads to a structured form of program that is relatively error free and easy to debug. This shall be discussed here also.

7-1. THE PROCEDURE SUBPROGRAM

We shall start by discussing a PASCAL subprogram called a PROCEDURE which is called by the main program when needed. For instance, suppose that we want to take the cube root of a variable at several points in a program. The following could be used.

```
PROGRAM SAMPLEPROC(INPUT,OUTPUT);
(*AN ILLUSTRATION OF A PROCEDURE SUBPROGRAM*)
VAR A,B,C,D:REAL;
PROCEDURE QBRT(VAR X,Y:REAL); (*PROCEDURE HEADING*)
VAR Q:REAL;
   BEGIN  (*START OF CUBE ROOT CALCULATION*)
      Q:=LN(X)/3.Ø;
      Y:=EXP(Q)
   END; (*END OF CUBE ROOT PROCEDURE*)                (7-1)
BEGIN (*START OF COMPUATIONS OF MAIN PROGRAM*)
   READLN(A);
   QBRT(A,B); (*CALL OF CUBE ROOT PROCEDURE*)
   C:=B*A;
   QBRT(C,D); (*ANOTHER CALL OF CUBE ROOT PROCEDURE*)
   WRITELN(D)
END.
```

Note the form of the program and of the PROCEDURE. The main program has its heading and declaration statements as usual (e.g. VAR, TYPE, LABEL). The PROCEDURE then follows. The first statement, called the PROCEDURE *heading* consists of the word PROCEDURE followed by an indentifier. A VAR statement follows which is enclosed in parentheses. The variables in the VAR statement represent either data that is to be supplied by the main program to the PROCEDURE, or data which the PROCEDURE supplies back to the main program. (We shall modify this subsequently.) Any variables that are used by the PROCEDURE alone, and are not to be passed back to the main program, are then declared. For instance, in PROCEDURE QBRT, Q is such a variable. Next the cube root is calculated, see Sec. 2-5. The END statement ends the PROCEDURE. The PROCEDURE appears before the calculations of the main program, so that when the compiler encounters a PROCEDURE call in the main program, it "knows" of the existence of the PROCEDURE.

Now, the main program commences. Data is read and assigned to A and the QBRT PROCEDURE is called. Note that this is done simply by writing the name followed by a list of variables, QBRT(X,Y). The variable list must be precisely the same as that in the PROCEDURE defining statement. That is, the variables must agree in number, type and order. For instance, if we have

```
PROCEDURE ABC(VAR X,Y:REAL;VAR I,J:INTEGER);        (7-2)
```

then, if we have a calling statement

```
ABC(E,F,G,H);                                                  (7-3)
```

E and F must have been declared REAL and G and H must have been declared INTEGER in the main program. Now, when the PROCEDURE is called, the variable called E will share a memory location with X; F will share a memory location with Y; G will share a memory location with I; and H will share a memory location with J. Hence, if F is changed in the PROCEDURE, Y will have this changed value when the main program commences. Note the repetition of VAR in (7-2). That is, when variables are declared in the calling statement, VAR must be repeated for each TYPE declared. (We shall modify this subsequently.) Now consider the variable Q which is declared REAL in the body of the PROCEDURE. This is called a *private variable*. Its value will not affect the value of any variable in the main program, even one that has the same name. (We shall discuss this subsequently.)

Now consider the main program. A value is entered and assigned to A. Now we have the call

```
QBRT(A,B);                                                     (7-4)
```

Now A and X will share a memory location and B and Y will share a memory location. Since the PROCEDURE only needs X as input, then the cube root is computed and stored in the memory location called B (or Y). Thus, the main program can use this value. Thus, the calculation for C:=B*A can be performed. Next the call

```
QBRT(C,D);
```

results in the cube root of C's being stored in the memory location called D. Hence, its value can be printed. Note that X and Y in the PROCEDURE are called *variable parameters*. They do not have memory locations of their own, but use the ones in the calling statement. For instance, in program (7-5), the first time that QBRT is called, X and A share the same memory location, while the second time that QBRT is called, X uses the memory location of C.

To illustrate the ideas of public and private values still further, let us consider the following modification of the program.

```
PROGRAM SAMPLEPROC2(INPUT,OUTPUT);
(*ILLUSTRATION OF PUBLIC AND PRIVATE VARIABLES
      IN A PROCEDURE SUBPROGRAM*)
```

```
VAR A,B,C,D,E,Q:REAL;
PROCEDURE QBRT(VAR X,Y:REAL);
  VAR Q:REAL; (*Q IS PRIVATE*)
    BEGIN (*START OF CUBE ROOT CALCULATION*)
      Q:=LN(X)/3.Ø                                        (7-5)
      Y:=EXP(Q);
      E:=Y (*E IS PUBLIC SINCE ONLY DECLARED IN
                       MAIN PROGRAM*)
    END; (*END OF CUBE ROOT PROCEDURE*)
BEGIN (*START OF COMPUTATIONS OF MAIN PROGRAM*)
  Q:=7; (*Q WILL NOT BE CHANGED BY PROCEDURE*)
  E:=9; (*E WILL BE CHANGED BY PROCEDURE*)
  READLN(A);
  QBRT(A,B); (*CALL OF CUBE ROOT PROCEDURE*)
  C:=B*A;
  QBRT(C,D); (*ANOTHER CALL OF CUBE ROOT PROCEDURE*)
  WRITELN(D);
  WRITELN(Q,E:15)
END.
```

This is the same as program (7-1) except that we have added two additional variables. Note that Q is declared both in the main program and in the PROCEDURE. However, Q is a private variable of the PROCEDURE so that the Q in the main program and the Q in the PROCEDURE have *nothing to do with each other.* The fact that their names are the *same* has *nothing* to do with the operation of the program (although it may confuse the programmer).

Now consider the variable E. It is used in the PROCEDURE but is not declared there. It is declared only in the main program. This is called a *public* or *global* variable. There is only one memory location called E and it is used by both the main program and the PROCEDURE. Thus, when E is changed by the PROCEDURE, it will also be changed when the main program is executed and vice versa.

As an example, suppose that when program (7-5) is run, we enter 8 for the value to be assigned to A. Then the following values will be printed out for the various variables.

D 2.51984

Q 7.ØØØ

E 2.51984

Note that Q is unchanged by the PROCEDURE while E is changed.

When data from the main program is supplied to the PROCEDURE or vice versa, the data is said to be *passed*. We have seen that variables in the main program can be passed to the PROCEDURE either by declaring them in the PROCEDURE heading or by using global variables. In either case, if the variable is changed in the PROCEDURE, it is also changed in the main program. Note that a global variable is different than one in the calling statement. A global variable only has one memory location, while the variable parameters in the PROCEDURE calling statement share memory locations only when the PROCEDURE is called. For instance, in program (7-5), at one point X and Y share memory locations with A and B, respectively. However, later in the execution, X and Y share memory locations with C and D, respectively, and not with A and B.

We can use global variables to pass all the variables from the main program to the PROCEDURE and vice versa. In such cases, there need be no parentheses and list in either the PROCEDURE heading or in the calling statements.

There are times when we want to pass a value from the main program to the PROCEDURE, but we do not want the PROCEDURE to be able to alter this value in the main program. One procedure for doing this is to avoid using that value on the left of an assignment statement. PASCAL also offers an alternative. If a value is listed in the list of the PROCEDURE heading *without* a VAR, then its value will be passed from the main program but it acts, otherwise, as a private variable. This is called a *value parameter*. As an example, consider program (7-6) where we have slightly modified program (7-5).

```
PROGRAM SAMPLEPROC2(INPUT,OUTPUT);
(*ILLUSTRATION OF GLOBAL AND PRIVATE VARIABLES
          IN A PROCEDURE SUBPROGRAM*)
VAR A,B,C,D,E,Q,R:REAL;
PROCEDURE QBRT(VAR X,Y:REAL;
                      Z:REAL);
   VAR Q:REAL;
   (*Q IS PRIVATE*)
   BEGIN (*START OF CUBE ROOT CALCULATIONS*)
      Q:=LN(X)/3.Ø;                                  (7-6)
      Y:=EXP(Q);
```

```
        Z:=2*Z; (*Z WILL NOT CHANGE CORRESPONDING
                   VARIABLE IN MAIN PROGRAM*)
        E:=Y (*E IS GLOBAL SINCE ONLY DECLARED IN
                   MAIN PROGRAM*)
    END; (*END OF CUBE ROOT CALCULATIONS*)
BEGIN (*START OF COMPUTATIONS IN MAIN PROGRAM*)
    Q:=7; (*Q WILL NOT BE CHANGED BY PROCEDURE*)
    E:=9; (*E WILL BE CHANGED BY PROCEDURE*)
    R:=4; (*R WILL NOT BE CHANGED BY PROCEDURE*)
    READLN(A);
    QBRT(A,B,R); (*CALL OF CUBE ROOT PROCEDURE*)
    C:=B*A;
    QBRT(C,D,R); (*ANOTHER CALL OF CUBE ROOT
                         PROCEDURE*)
    WRITELN(D);
    WRITELN(Q,E:15);
    WRITELN(R)
END.
```

Note the variable Z in the opening statement of PROCEDURE QBRT. Since there is no VAR preceding it here, Z is a value parameter. Note the calling statement

```
QBRT(A,B,R);
```

The value of R will be passed to Z. However, Z and R represent different memory locations so, even if Z is changed in the PROCEDURE, the value of R is not changed in the main program. (Note that the value of Z can be changed in the PROCEDURE.) As an example, if the data entered assigned 8 to A, then the following values will be printed.

D	2.51984
Q	7
E	2.51984
R	4

A syntax diagram for the PROCEDURE heading is shown in Fig. 7-1. The ability to have private variables is very important. A collection of PROCEDURES can be stored in a library and the programmer (or other programmers) can use these PROCEDURES as part of a main program without having to worry if there is a conflict of names or if the PROCEDURE will change any values in the main program.

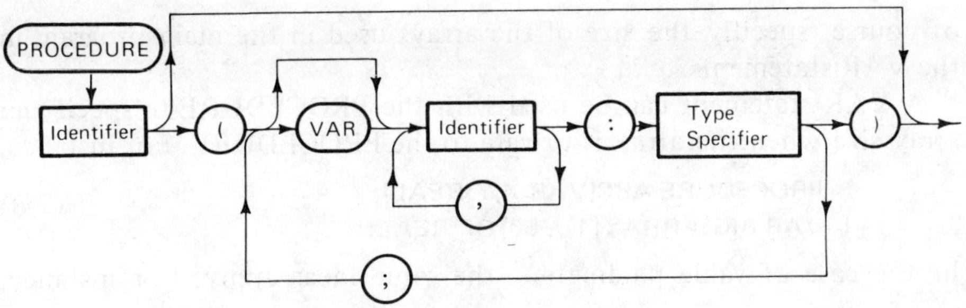

Figure 7-1. Syntax diagram for PROCEDURE heading

7-2. USE OF PROCEDURES WITH ARRAYS

Information concerning arrays can be passed back and forth between the PROCEDURE and the main program. If the array name appears as a variable parameter or as a value parameter, then the entire array can be passed just by listing its name. As an illustration, consider the following program.

```
PROGRAM PROCARRTEST(INPUT,OUTPUT);
(*ILLUSTRATION OF ARRAYS WITH PROCEDURES*)
TYPE MAT=ARRAY[1 . . 5Ø] OF REAL;
VAR A:ARRAY[1 . . 5Ø] OF REAL;
      I,M:INTEGER;
  PROCEDURE ARMULT(VAR X:MAT;
                            J:INTEGER);                  (7-7)
  VAR K:INTEGER;
     BEGIN
        FOR K:=1 TO J DO X[K]:=K*X[K] ;
     END; (*END OF PROCEDURE*)
BEGIN
   READLN(M);
   FOR I:= 1 TO M DO A[I] :=I;
   ARMULT(A,M);
   FOR I:=1 TO M DO WRITELN(A[I] :1Ø)
END.
```

Note that the size specification is *not* included in the list of the PROCEDURE heading. That is, a TYPE statement *must* be used in the main program to establish a TYPE for the array used. The main program can, of course, specifiy the size of the arrays used in the main program in the VAR statements.

A VAR statement can be used with the PROCEDURE to specify an array size when the array is private to the PROCEDURE. For instance,

```
PROCEDURE ABC(VAR X,Y:REAL);                    (7-8)
VAR BIG:ARRAY[1 . . 5Ø] OF REAL;
```

In the case of value parameters, the same ideas apply. For instance,

```
TYPE MAT=ARRAY[1 . . 5Ø] OF REAL;
   .                                            (7-9)
   .
PROCEDURE ABC(VAR X:MAT;Y:MAT);
```

Now X and Y are arrays which are passed to the procedure by the main program, but the PROCEDURE cannot change the value of the matrix passed to Y by the main program. For instance, if we have CALL(A,B) then the A array can be changed in the main program by the PROCEDURE but the B array cannot.

The arrays that we have discussed are *not* packed. Many compilers will not allow the use of packed arrays as variable parameters or as value parameters although individual elements can be used. Note that global variables can be packed arrays with most compilers.

7-3. THE FUNCTION SUBPROGRAM

A PROCEDURE can be used to compute many values and return them to the main program. There are times when we wnat to compute only one value. In such cases, there is an operation called the FUNCTION that can be more convenient to use than the PROCEDURE. We have already dealt with library FUNCTIONS, see Sec. 2-5. For instance, if we use the library FUNCTION to take the square root of a variable X, we need only write

```
Y:=SQRT(X);                                     (7-1Ø)
```

In PASCAL, the programmer can write his own FUNCTIONS and use them in the same way as library FUNCTIONS. For instance, the following program illustrates a FUNCTION that takes the cube root of a variable.

```
PROGRAM SAMPLEFUNCTION(INPUT,OUTPUT);
(*ILLUSTRATION OF A FUNCTION*)
```

```
VAR A,B,C:REAL;
   FUNCTION QBRT(X:REAL):REAL; (*FUNCTION HEADING*)
   VAR Q:REAL;                                      (7-11)
   BEGIN
      Q:=LN(X)/3.Ø;
      QBRT:=EXP(Q)
   END;
BEGIN (*MAIN PROGRAM COMPUTATIONS*)
   READLN(A);
   B:=QBRT(A)*A;
   C:=QBRT(B);
   WRITELN(C)
END.
```

The FUNCTION heading consists of the word FUNCTION followed by an identifier that is the FUNCTION name. This is followed by a pair of parentheses containing a list of variables. This is followed by a colon and a TYPE identifier. The list of variables is the same as that for the PROCEDURE. The FUNCTION returns a single answer under its own name. Thus, a FUNCTION must be declared as to TYPE. This is done by writing a colon and TYPE specifier after the parentheses in the FUNCTION heading. A syntax diagram for the FUNCTION heading is shown in Fig. 7-2.

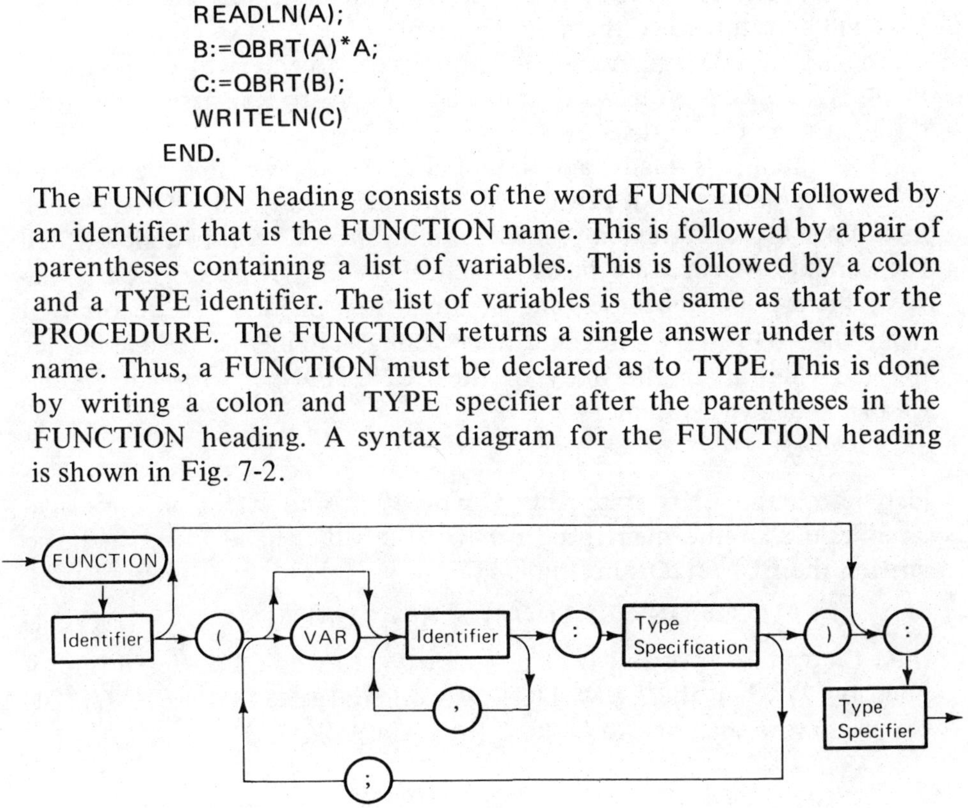

Figure 7-2. Syntax diagram for a FUNCTION heading

The body of the FUNCTION then follows the heading. At some point in the body of the FUNCTION, the FUNCTION name must be assigned a value. For instance, in program (7-11) we have the statement

```
QBRT:=LN(X)/3.Ø;                                    (7-12)
```

This, then, is the value which will be returned to the main program.

The FUNCTION is called just as is a library FUNCTION. For instance, in program (7-11), we have

```
B:=QBRT(Z)*A;
```
(7-13a)

and

```
C:=QBRT(B);
```
(7-13b)

Note that, in a FUNCTION, the name must be assigned a value at least once. It may be done more than once, but the last statement executed containing the FUNCTION name will provide the value that will be returned to the main program.

The FUNCTION name should not appear to the right of an assignment sign, unless you want the FUNCTION to call itself. We shall discuss this in the next section.

The statements made about global variables, variable parameters, value parameters, and private variable also apply to FUNCTIONS, including those statements made about arrays. For instance, if all the variables needed are passed to the FUNCTION using global variables, then the parentheses and all that they include can be omitted from the FUNCTION heading and calling statements. Also consider the fact that if, in the body of the FUNCTION of program (7-11), we had added the statement

```
X:=2*X
```

just before the END statement, it would have no effect on the calculated values of the main program. On the other hand, if we had also written the FUNCTION heading as

```
FUNCTION QBRT(VAR X:REAL):REAL;
```
(7-14)

then the values of A and B in program (7-11) would be altered (multiplied by 2) when the FUNCTION was called. (Note that a FUNCTION can pass more than one variable to the main program.)

7-4. RECURSIVE USE OF SUBPROGRAMS

A PROCEDURE or FUNCTION can call other PROCEDURES and FUNCTIONS. If a PROCEDURE or FUNCTION calls itself, this is termed a *recursive* use of the subprogram. To illustrate this, let us perform the calculation of the power series

$$C = 1 + \frac{1}{X} + \frac{1}{X^2} + \frac{1}{X^3} + \ldots \qquad (7\text{-}15)$$

The calculation of such an infinite series would require an infinite amount of time. Thus, we usually terminate the operation when the last term becomes small enough. (The subject of the convergence of infinite series is related to the determination of how small is "small enough". This is beyond the scope of this book.) Let us assume that we will terminate the execution when $1/x^n$ becomes less than ∅.∅∅∅∅∅1. A program that accomplishes this using a recursive PROCEDURE call follows.

```
PROGRAMRECURSIVEPROC(INPUT,OUTPUT);
(*RECURSIVE CALCULATION OF A SERIES SIGMA 1/X TO N*)
VAR X,C:REAL;
   PROCEDURE SER(A:REAL);
   BEGIN
      A:=A*A;
      C:=C+A;
      IF(A>Ø.ØØØØØ1)THEN SER(A) (*RECURSIVE CALL OF
                                          PROCEDURE*)
   END;
BEGIN                                                   (7-16)
   READLN(X);
   X:=1/X;
   C:=1.Ø+X;
   SER(X);
   WRITELN(C)
END.
```

The PROCEDURE inputs a value A and then multiplies it by itself. The result is then assigned to A which is then added to a global variable C. If A>∅.∅∅∅∅∅1, then the PROCEDURE calls itself. The new value of A is again obtain by multiplying the valued assigned in A by itself, and this is added to C. This processs repeats until the calculated value of A becomes equal to or less than ∅.∅∅∅∅∅1.

Consider the main program. X is entered and replaced by 1/X. Then we form

$$C{:=}1 + \frac{1}{X}$$

After the first pass through the PROCEDURE, we have $C = 1 + (1/X) + (1/X^2)$. With each successive pass, an additional term in the series is added until the desired series is completed. Note that this is neither the most efficient nor the most convenient means of calculatating the desired series. It is merely used as an illustration of the recursive process.

When a recursive program is written, care should be taken to avoid an endless loop. For instance, in program (7-16), if the IF-THEN statement were not included, the procedure would call itself endlessly. This may result in an error which would terminate execution without the wasting of too much computer time. However, such operation should be avoided.

FUNCTIONS can also be used recursively. For instance, consider the following program.

```
PROGRAM SAMPLEFUNCTION(INPUT,OUTPUT);
(*ILLUSTRATION OF A FUNCTION USED RECURSIVELY*)
VAR A,B:REAL;
   FUNCTION QBRT(X:REAL):REAL;
   VAR Q:REAL;
   BEGIN
      Q:=LN(X)/3.Ø;                                  (7-17)
      X:=2.Ø*X;
      Q:=EXP(Q);
      IF Q>1.999 THEN Q:=QBRT(Q);
      QBRT:=Q
   END;
BEGIN (*MAIN PROGRAM COMPUTATIONS*)
   READLN(A);
   B:=QBRT(A);
   WRITELN(B)
END.
```

This utilizes the cube root FUNCTION of program (7-11). However, now, if the calculated value of Q is greater than 1.999, the QBRT FUNCTION is called again. Thus, the ninth root is taken. This procedure repeats until the value returned is equal to or less then 1.999. With many PASCAL compilers we cannot use the same FUNCTION name on both sides of an assignment sign. Thus, the "dummy" variable Q must be used here.

7-5. NESTED SUBPROGRAMS

A subprogram can call other subprograms that are external to it. However, there are times when it is desirable to write a completely self-contained subprogram. In such cases, any FUNCTIONS or PROCEDURES that the subprogram calls should lie entirely within itself (i.e. that subprogram). This is called *nesting* of subprograms. For instance,

```
PROGRAM NESTEDSUBPROGRAMS(INPUT,OUTPUT);
(*ILLUSTRATION OF NESTED SUBPROGRAMS*)
VAR A,B,C:REAL;
   PROCEDURE COMBINE(VAR X:REAL;Y,Z:REAL);
      FUNCTION QBRT(W:REAL):REAL; (*NESTED FUNCTION
                                               STARTS*)
      VAR Q:REAL;
      BEGIN
         Q:=LN(W)/3.Ø;                                    (7-18)
         QBRT:=EXP(Q)
      END; (*NESTED FUNCTION ENDS*)
   BEGIN (*BODY OF MAIN PROCEDURE STARTS*)
      Y:=2.Ø*Z*Y;
      X:=4*QBRT(Y);
      X:=QBRT(X)+4.Ø
   END; (*END OF MAIN PROCEDURE*)
BEGIN (*MAIN PROGRAM STARTS*)
   READLN(A,B);
   COMBINE(C,A,B);
   WRITELN(C);
   A:=2*A;
   COMBINE(C,A,A);
   WRITELN(C)
END.
```

Here the FUNCTION QBRT is nested within the PROCEDURE COMBINE. The rules for writing a nested subprogram are essentially the same as those for writing a main program and subprogram. The nested subprogram must start and end before the BEGIN statement of the outer subprogram. The declaration statements of the outer subprogram (LABEL, TYPE, VAR, etc.) can precede the beginning of the nested subprogram, just as those for a main program can precede those for a subprogram. The rules for global and private variables, etc. apply here as before.

There can be several degrees of nesting, that is, one subprogram can be nested within a second, which can be nested within a third, etc.

Your computer manual should be checked to determine the degree of nesting allowed.

The main program *cannot* call a nested subprogram. Similarly, if there are many degrees of nesting, a nested subprogram cannot be called from outside of the subprogram within which it is nested.

7-6. FORWARD REFERENCES

A PROCEDURE or FUNCTION can call another subprogram. However, a subprogram should be listed in the program *before* it is called so that the compiler "knows" of its existence. At times it may be inconvenient or impossible to do this. For instance, two subprograms may call each other recursively and we cannot write both of them first. For program organization, it may be desirable to write certain subprograms before others. There is a PASCAL statement called a FORWARD *reference* that allows us to circumvent these difficulties. Its use is illustrated in program (7-19).

```
PROGRAM FORWARDSUBPROGRAM(INPUT,OUTPUT);
(*ILLUSTRATION OF A FORWARD REFERENCE*)
VAR A,B,C:REAL;
    I,J,K:INTEGER;
FUNCTION QBRT(X:REAL):REAL;FORWARD;(*FORWARD
                                       REFERENCE*)
PROCEDURE COMP(VAR Y:REAL;Z:REAL); (*HEADING OF
                                   PROCEDURE COMP*)
  BEGIN
    Y:=2*QBRT(X)
  END; (*END OF PROCEDURE COMP*)                    (7-19)
FUNCTION QBRT; (*THE BODY OF QBRT STARTS*)
  VAR Q:REAL;
    BEGIN
      Q:=LN(X)/3.Ø;
      QBRT:=EXP(Q)
    END; (*END OF FUNCTION QBRT*)
BEGIN (*START OF MAIN PROGRAM*)
  READLN(A);
  COMP(B,A);
  WRITELN(B)
END.
```

The PROCEDURE COMP calls the FUNCTION QBRT. Suppose that we want to write COMP before QBRT. To do this we write the heading of QBRT with the expression ;FORWARD added to it, *before* the PROCEDURE COMP. The PROCEDURE COMP is then written. We then start QBRT with a subheading which consists only of the word FUNCTION and the name (in this case, QBRT). Next, the body of the FUNCTION is written.

We have illustrated the use of a FORWARD reference with a FUNCTION. The same form is used with a PROCEDURE. For instance,

```
    :
PROCEDURE ABC(VAR A:REAL;B:REAL);FORWARD;
    :                                              (7-2Ø)
PROCEDURE ABC; (*SUBHEADING*)
    :
END;
    :
```

At times, a programmer writes a FUNCTION or PROCEDURE and then stores it in a library. The library may actually contain many programs which have been written by many programmers. Such subprograms can also be used by appropriately referencing them. The mode of reference varies from compiler to compiler and your manual should be checked to determine the exact form. Often, the word EXTERN is used. For instance, suppose that there is a PROCEDURE in the library called NETWORKS. If you want to use it in your program, then the statement

```
PROCEDURE NETWORKS(VAR X,Y,Z:REAL;
                   M,N:REAL);EXTERN          (7-21)
```

must be written. That is, you write the PROCEDURE (or FUNCTION) heading followed by a semicolon and the word EXTERN. When the program is run, the specified subprogram will be obtained from the library and will be added to your program, just as if you had written it there yourself. Note that you must know the proper form of the subprogram heading. Remember that the procedures for putting subprograms into a library as well as those for referencing them are not standard and your computer manual should be checked before the operation is attempted.

7-7. PROCEDURE AND FUNCTION PARAMETERS

Some compilers allow the passing of PROCEDURES and FUNCTIONS as *variables* to other subprograms. For instance, suppose that we have a subprogram and the first time that it is called, we want to take the cube root of a variable. The next time that the subprogram is called, we want the fifth root instead of the cube root. Suppose that there are two FUNCTIONS, QBRT(X:REAL) and FIVRT(X:REAL) which have either been written in the program or are library FUNCTIONS. We can use the procedures illustrated by the following program segment.

```
    :
FUNCTION QBRT(X:REAL):REAL;
    :
END;
FUNCTION FIVRT(X:REAL);
    :
END;                                                    (7-22)
    :
PROCEDURE TEST(FUNCTION A,B:REAL;VAR Q:REAL;Z:REAL);
VAR I,J,K:REAL;
    :
I:=A(Z);
J:=B(I);
    :
END;
BEGIN
   TEST(QBRT,QBRT,TIME,VELOCITY);
    :
   TEST(FIVRT,FIVRT,DISTANCE,SPEED);
```

Now A and B are variables, but will become FUNCTION names. For instance, the first time that TEST is called, the statements

```
I:=A(Z);                                                (7-23)
J:=B(I);
```

will be executed as

```
I:=QBRT(Z);
J:=QBRT(I);
```

The second time that TEST is called, the statements in question will be executed as

```
I:=FIVRT(Z);
J:=FIVRT(I);
```

Note that the expression in the parentheses following A and B must be appropriate to the list of the FUNCTION (or PROCEDURE) that is to be executed. Using the technique discussed here the *name* of the FUNCTION can be passed as a parameter just as a variable is. In a similar way, the name of a PROCEDURE can be passed. The operations discussed in this section are not standard on all PASCAL compilers and, thus, your computer manual should be checked before attempting to use them.

7-8. STRUCTURED PROGRAMMING—MODULARIZATION—TOP DOWN PROGRAMMING

The use of subprograms allows the writing of modular programs. That is, a long complex program can be written as a series of subprograms. Such programs are simpler to write and debug because the task is broken up into simple subjobs. The subprograms are called *modules*.

Top Down Design

We can use modularization in conjunction with a procedure called *top down design* to easily write programs that usually have fewer errors and can be easily debugged. Using this procedure, the program is written as a main program which calls subprograms, or modules. Usually, very little computation is performed in the main program and most of the computation is done in the modules. Of course, *when the original algorithm is written, this plan must be considered*. The general program structure can be represented by a diagram called a *hierarchy diagram*. A typical one is shown in Fig. 7-3. Here the main program calls upon the modules a, b and c. In addition, module a calls upon modules d and e, while modules b and c call upon module e.

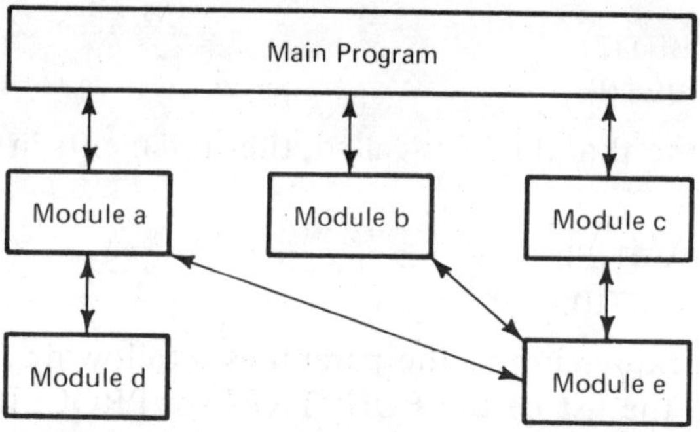

Figure 7-3. A simple hierarchical diagram

Top down design consists of more than simply modularization of the program. The programming is performed in a special way. The main program is written first. It is tested *before* the subprograms are written. To do this, the actual subprograms are replaced with very simple ones called *stubs*. The stubs simply test to see if the data is passed correctly. For instance, the stubs would have WRITELN statements in them to make sure that the data is passed properly. After the main program is written and checked, each module is written and tested in turn. This should first be done without the main program in order to isolate a bug if it occurs. That is, a very simple "main program" is written to test the subprogram. If the module runs properly, then it is tested with the main program. If the module and the main program run properly, then the next module is written and checked, etc.

Let us illustrate this procedure in conjunction with Fig. 7-3. First, the main program would be written and tested with three stubs. Next, subprogram a would be written and tested with two stubs, representing modules d and e. Then it would be tested with the main program. Modules b and c would be developed in the same way.

Next, subprogram d would be written and, after being tested by itself, it would be tested with subprogram a and the main program. Similarly, subprogram e is written, tested by itself, and then tested with subprograms a, b, and c and the main program. Finally, the entire program is tested. Note that, at each stage, the subprograms are tested by themselves and that the program then is tested whenever modules are added. Therefore, if an error occurs, it will probably be in a small module and, thus, will be easy to debug. Note that it is desirable for modules to be kept small. In general, a module should be less than two pages long, if possible.

7-9. DEBUGGING PROGRAMS

The procedure discussed in the last section usually results in programs that are relatively free of bugs. However, bugs occur in almost all programs no matter how experienced the programmer. The beginning programmer may become discouraged because of bugs, but this should not be the case. *Debugging should be considered to be a part of programming.*

In general, bugs can be divided into two categories. The first type is detected during compilation while the second is detected during or after execution. If the rules of syntax are violated, then the program will not compile. On the other hand, the program may be perfectly good PASCAL and still produce problems. There can be a logical error (e.g. C:=A−B; may be written instead of C:=A+B;), in which case, answers will be obtained but they will be wrong. Other errors can occur during execution. For instance, suppose that we have INT:=INT1*INT2; where all quantities are integers. If INT1=1Ø,5ØØ and INT2=26,ØØØ, then the product will be too large for most computers to handle and an overflow will result causing computation to cease.

Debugging of Errors Detected During Compilation

When the syntax of PASCAL is violated, compilation ceases and an error message results. This error message points to that statement which is " in error." If this is actually the case, then the error can usually be quickly corrected. On the other hand, the "accused" statement is often innocent of an error. For instance, if you forgot to declare a variable, then the first time that the variable name appears, an error message will be given. Forgetting to write a BEGIN statement at the end of the declaration part of the program can produce several unexpected error messages. You may want to size two arrays identically but, inadvertently, you do not do so. If you subsequently assign the value of one array to the other, an error message will result. In general, experience with your compiler will lead to a facility for using the error messages and make the debugging of syntax errors easier. Careful reading of the program often detects syntax errors.

Debugging of Error Detected During Execution

A compiled program may not run due to the fact that the values become too large or too small. That is, an overflow or an underflow results. If the answers are actually too large or too small, then this is a true overflow (or underflow). On the other hand, sometimes these problems can be avoided by thoughtful programming. For instance, suppose that we perform the calculation

$$x = (a/b)c \tag{7-24}$$

where a = 156,783, b = Ø.13 × 1Ø$^{-37}$ and c = Ø.37 × 1Ø$^{-36}$. Suppose that the largest number that can be handled by the computer is 1Ø^{38}. If we calculate a/b and then multiply by c, an overflow will result since a/b > 1Ø^{38}. On the other hand, if we calculate a/c and then multiply the result by b, no problem will result since the results of all the calculations remain within bounds. At times, such simple manipulations can avoid the problems of overflow and underflow. On the other hand, there are times when relatively complex procedures must be used.

There are times when a logically correct program produces erroneous results because of roundoff errors. When there are a great many calculaions, a small error in each calculation may often result in an unacceptably large error in the final answer. In such cases, sophisticated programming techniques may have to be used, but sometimes simple manipulations are helpful. Let us illustrate some basic ideas. Suppose that we want to calculate

$$v = q[(f/f_0) - (f_0/f)] \tag{7-25}$$

where q = 1ØØ, f_0 = 1Ø^6 and f = 1Ø^6 − 1. Since f/f_0 and f_0/f will both be very close to 1, a small error in either term can result in a large percentage error in v. Hence, a statement such as

```
V:=Q*(F/FØ – FØ/F);                                    (7-26)
```

is prone to large roundoff errors. On the other hand, we might know the difference between f_0 and f very accurately. We can represent it as

$$\delta = f - f_0 \tag{7-27}$$

We can improve the accuracy by expression the results in terms of δ. For instance, noting that

$$f/f_0 = 1 + (\delta/f_0)$$

and substituting in Eq. (7-25), we have

$$v = \frac{1 + (\delta^2/f_0{}^2) + (2\delta/f_0) - 1}{1 + (\delta/f_0)} \tag{7-28}$$

Note that the subtraction 1 − 1 can be performed *exactly* and we have

$$v = \frac{q[(\delta^2/f_0{}^2) + (2\delta/f_0)]}{1 + (\delta/f_0)} = q(\delta/f_0)\frac{[(\delta/f_0) + 2]}{[(\delta/f_0) + 1]} \qquad (7\text{-}29)$$

We no longer have to obtain the difference between two nearly equal numbers. Thus, a PASCAL statement that would exhibit much less roundoff error than statement (7-26) is

```
V:=Q*(DELTA/FØ)*(DELTA/FØ+2.Ø)/(1+DELTA/FØ);          (7-3Ø)
```

It is assumed that the value of DELTA is known prior to the execution of this statement. In general, a study of the algebraic relations in the algorithm can lead to programs which minimize roundoff error. At times, however, such procedures may become very sophisticated.

Logical Errors

There are times when a program runs but does not compute what you want it to. There is a logical bug. One way to debug such a program is to perform all the calculations by hand and see what the intermediate answers are. Next, add extra WRITE statements to the program which print out the intermediate results. These should be checked with the results of the hand calculations. In this way, the location of the bug(s) can be isolated. If this does not locate all of the bugs, then step out the program "just as the computer does." This will usually indicate the bug. Once the error is eliminated, the extra WRITE statements should be removed.

Remember that all programs should be checked using several sets of known data. *You should never assume that a program is logically correct no matter how simple it is.*

EXERCISES

1. Discuss the operation of the following program

```
PROGRAM TEST(INPUT,OUTPUT);
VAR A,B,C,D:REAL;
   PROCEDURE ABC(VAR X,Y:REAL;Z:REAL);
   VAR M:REAL;
      BEGIN
         M:=Z+D;
         Y:=2*M;
         X:=M+Y;
```

```
        D:=D+1
      END;
BEGIN
  A:=3.Ø;
  D:=4.Ø;
  ABC(B,C,A);
  WRITELN(A,B,C,D)
END.
```

Check the results by running the program on your computer.

2. Write a PROCEDURE that averages 5 quantities. Check your results by writing a main program for the PROCEDURE and running the entire program on your computer.
3. Discuss global and private variables and variable and value parameters.
4. Write a PROCEDURE, using an array, that enters N numbers and obtains their average. Check your program by writing a main program and then running the combined program on your computer.
5. Write a PROCEDURE that finds the largest value in an array. Check your program by writing a main program and running the combined program on your computer.
6. Write a PROCEDURE that alphabetizes a list of names. Check your program by writing a main program and running the combined program on your computer.
7. Write a procedure that finds the root of the equation Ø.5 − sin x = Ø. Check your program by writing a main program and running the combined program on your computer.
8. Repeat Exericse 2 but now use a FUNCTION.
9. Repeat Exercise 4 but now use a FUNCTION.
1Ø. Repeat Exercise 5 but now use a FUNCTION.
11. Repeat Exercise 7 but now use a FUNCTION.
12. Use recursive calls to evaluate

$$f(x) + [1/(2x^2)] + [1/(2x^4)] + \ldots$$

Cease computation when a term becomes less than a number which is to be input by the user. Check the program by running it on your computer.

13. Repeat Exercise 12 but now evaluate

$$f(x) = \sin^2 x + \sin^3 x + \ldots$$

14. Write a program using nested subprograms that orders a list of numbers and then prints their average. Check your program by writing a main program and running the combined program on your computer.
15. Discuss the use of FORWARD references. Write a program that uses a FORWARD reference and check it on your computer.
16. Write a FUNCTION using subprograms that call each other and which evaluates

$$Z = [[[X+Y]^{1/2}]^{1/3}]^{1/2}$$

17. Write a FUNCTION that calculates x^y. Check your program by writing a main program and running the combined program on your computer.
18. What is meant by top down programming?
19. Discuss the various types of bugs that can occur in a program.
20. How can logical bugs be corrected?
21. Why should a program always be checked using several sets of data?

Chapter Eight

Additional TYPE Specifications—Files

In this chapter we shall discuss some additional TYPE statements that can be of help in making programs both more readable and self-documenting. We shall also consider the important topic of sequential files in which much data can be stored and accessed. We start by discussing an extension of the data TYPES that we have already discussed.

8-1. USER DEFINED TYPES

We have worked with various scalar TYPES. (A *scalar* is a single variable, not an array.) These include REAL, INTEGER, CHAR and BOOLEAN. These are specifically defined as part of the PASCAL language. In addition, PASCAL allows the programmer to define certain types of variables. For instance, suppose that we are working with a program that computes a person's salary, which varies according to the days that he works. We could define a variable TYPE called DAY which has the components SUN, MON, TUES, WED, THURS, FRI, and SAT. A statement that would do this is

```
TYPE DAY=(SUN,MON,TUES,WED,
          THURS,FRI,SAT);                    (8-1)
```

The form of the statement is the word TYPE followed by an identifier and an = sign. Following this is a list of *all* the elements of the new TYPE enclosed in parentheses. The order in which the elements are listed is important. We shall discuss this subsequently. Once the TYPE is established we can use the VAR statement in the usual way.

```
VAR A,B:DAY;                                 (8-2)
```

Now A and B will be variables of TYPE DAY. (Note that the word DAY is arbitrary; it is just a convenient one to use. We could just as easily have used ABCD.) Since A is of TYPE DAY, we can now perform some (but not all) of the PASCAL operations using it. For instance, we can use the assignment

```
A:=TUES;                                                    (8-3)
```

Now A would be assigned the value TUES.

These are a limited number of operations that can be performed with user defined TYPES. Each element of the TYPE is given an ordinal number which is determined by its order in the original TYPE specification. These ordinal numbers allow the library FUNCTIONS ORD, SUCC, and PRED to be used. For instance, consider the following program.

```
PROGRAM DEFINEDATA(INPUT,OUTPUT);
(*SAMPLE OF USER DEFINED DATA TYPE*)
TYPE DAY=(SUN,MON,TUES,WED,THURS,FRI,SAT);
     WEEKDAY=MON .. FRI;
VAR WORK,COUNTER:DAY;
     SUB,PART:WEEKDAY;                                      (8-4)
BEGIN
   FOR COUNTER:=SUN TO SAT DO WRITE(ORD(COUNTER));
   WORK:=TUES;
   WRITELN;
   WRITELN(ORD(SUCC(WORK)));
   WRITELN(ORD(PRED(WORK)));
   IF WORK=TUES THEN WRITELN(' TRUE');
   FOR SUB:=MON TO FRI DO WRITE(ORD(SUB));
   WRITELN
END.
```

When the program is run, the following values will be printed:

```
0 1 2 3 4 5 6
  3
  1
TRUE
1 2 3 4 5
```

For the moment, ignore the WEEKDAY reference. Let us consider the FOR-DO loop.

```
FOR COUNTER:=SUN TO SAT DO;                                  (8-5)
```

This illustrates that a user defined scalar can be used as an index in a FOR-DO loop. For this application, user defined COUNTER will take on SUN, MON, . . . , SAT in succession. Of course, COUNTER *must* be declared to be of TYPE DAY.

The statement WRITE(ORD(COUNTER)); causes the ordinal values of SUN, MON, . . . , SAT to be printed out. Note that these are Ø, 1, 2, . . . , 6. The ordinal numbers will always be assigned to user defined TYPE variables in the *order* in which they were originally written. Note that some compilers may start with 1 rather than with Ø.

Now consider the statement

```
IF WORK=TUES THEN . . .                                      (8-6)
```

This illustrates that user defined scalars can be used with the BOOLEAN relational operators. Note that *all* the BOOLEAN relational operators can be used, and that the comparison is based upon the ordinal values.

Note that when we set WORK:=TUES, then ORD(SUCC(WORK)) is 3 (corresponding to WED) and ORD(PRED(WORK)) is 2 (corresponding to MON). Although we can use the FUNCTION ORD, we cannot use the CHR FUNCTION with user defined variables.

We can also define a *subrange* of variables. For instance, in program (8-4) we define the subrange, weekdays, after the TYPE statement, by writing

```
WEEKDAY=MON . . FRI;                                         (8-7)
```

This means that WEEKDAY is not a new TYPE, since a range of values, rather than a complete list of values enclosed in parentheses, is given. The . . indicates all values between the listed "endpoints." When a subrange is listed, the ordinal values of its elements are those of the TYPE. This is also illustrated by the results of program (8-4).

We could also define a subrange of other variables. For instance if, under a TYPE statement, we wrote

```
COUNT=1 . . 7;                                               (8-8)
```

then COUNT would be a subrange of TYPE INTEGER that could only take on the values 1, 2, 3, . . , 7. This might be an advantage in that it would save storage space. Note that the *maximum* allowed size of the integers used determines the number of bits required to store *any* integer. Limiting the range that a variable can take on can also avoid some other problems which we shall discuss subsequently.

As a further illustration of user defined TYPE, let us write a program that computes the amount of pay a worker receives per day. We shall assume that the hourly rate varies with the day of the week. The program is

```
PROGRAM DAYSPAY(INPUT,OUTPUT);
(*SAMPLE OF COMPUTATION USING USER DEFINED
                          DATA TYPE*)
TYPE DAY=(SUN,MON,TUES,WED,THURS,FRI,SAT);
     COUNT=1 . . 7;
VAR WORK:DAY;
     I:COUNT;
     HOURS,PAY:REAL;                                  (8-9)
BEGIN
   READLN(I,HOURS);
   IF I=1 THEN WORK:=SUN
      ELSE IF I=2 THEN WORK:=MON
         ELSE IF I=3 THEN WORK:=TUES
            ELSE IF I=4 THEN WORK:=WED
               ELSE IF I=5 THEN WORK:=THURS
                  ELSE IF I=6 THEN WORK:=FRI
                     ELSE IF I=7 THEN WORK:=SAT;
   CASE WORK OF
      SUN:PAY:=HOURS*15.22;
      MON:PAY:=HOURS*7.15;
      TUES:PAY:=HOURS*8.57;
      WED:PAY:=HOURS*8.ØØ;
      THURS:PAY:=HOURS*8.5Ø;
      FRI:PAY:=HOURS*9.5Ø;
      SAT:PAY:=HOURS*15.22
   END;
   WRITELN(' DAYS PAY IS',PAY:7:2)
END.
```

Note that we declare variables of type DAY to be the days of the week and that COUNT is a subrange of the TYPE INTEGER. Then WORK is declared to be a variable of TYPE DAY, I is declared to be of TYPE COUNT, and HOURS and PAY are of TYPE REAL. The data that is entered is a number corresponding to the day of the week and the hours worked. Note that since we cannot read or write with user defined scalars, we use an INTEGER to specify the day. The multiple IF-THEN-ELSE statement then sets the variable WORK equal to the day worked.

Next we have a CASE statement. Note that the user defined scalar can be used as the selection variable in a CASE statement. The day's pay is then computed by the appropriate branch of the CASE statement.

The use of the subrange for integers can avoid problems. For instance, if an integer not of the subrange (i.e. other than 1, 2, . . . 7) were entered, many PASCAL compilers would print an error message and incorrect computations would not be performed. Thus, it is desirable to use the subrange here. (Unfortunately, not all PASCAL compilers will print an error message under these circumstances and undetected incorrect results may occur.)

It may seem as though the use of user defined scalars is more trouble than it is worth, since we could use the INTEGER I as the CASE selection variable and would not have to write the multiple IF-THEN-ELSE statement. However, the use of user defined scalars makes the program self-documenting. In larger programs, this can be an important feature. All programs should be documented but the temptation is not to do so. Making the program self-documenting can avoid problems, especially if you come back to a program after some time has elapsed. That is, if you see MON you know that it represents the day of the week. A 1 may not be immediately obvious to the programmer and time would be wasted in studying the program to determine the meaning of the statements.

Note that the operations allowed with user defined data TYPES are limited. The ones that are available on most compilers have been discussed here. The other PASCAL operations are usually not allowed.

8-2. SEQUENTIAL DATA FILES

Often, the data obtained during the running of a program must be stored for use at a later time. For instance, suppose that a list of names and grades is input. We might sort the list alphabetically. The data would be updated from time to time and then, at some later date, the entire list might be printed. This information would not be stored in the memory of the computer. Rather, it would be stored on magnetic media such as disks or tape. Such data is often stored in a *sequential data file* which is one where the characters are read and written in sequence. In order to obtain an individual piece of data, the entire file, up to the desired date, must be read.

A simple program that creates a file and writes to it follows.

```
PROGRAM INTDATFILE(INPUT,OUTPUT,INFO);
VAR INFO:FILE OF INTEGER;
    I,J:INTEGER;
BEGIN                                          (8-1Ø)
  REWRITE(INFO,'#9:INT.DATA');
  FOR I:=1 TO 1Ø DO
    BEGIN
      READ(J);
      INFO↑:=J; PUT(INFO)
    END;
  CLOSE(INFO,LOCK)
END.
```

In this program, the file is called INFO. Note that we list its name in the program title. (We shall discuss this in Sec. 8-5.) The FILE is actually created with the VAR statement which declares INFO to be a FILE of INTEGER. We can also have a FILE of REAL, FILE of BOOLEAN, FILE of CHAR, etc. A FILE can only be of one TYPE. We must use several files to store data of different TYPES. Figure 8-1 shows a syntax diagram for a FILE definition. Although the file is

Figure 8-1. Syntax diagram for a FILE specification

declared in the VAR statement, it must also be opened on the storage medium. The REWRITE statement does this. Its form is

```
REWRITE(File name, 'Destination');             (8-11)
```

The REWRITE statement causes a file of the specified name to be opened on the destination medium. For instance, consider the statement

```
REWRITE(INFO,'#9:INT.DATA');                   (8-12)
```

INFO is the name of the file as far as the program is concerned. #9: INT.DATA is its destination. The form of the destination will vary from computer to computer. In (8-12), #9 refers to a particular floppy disk drive. INT.DATA is the name we have chosen to assign to the particular file on the floppy disk. The file will be stored on the floppy disk under the name INT.DATA. On large computers, the file may be automatically placed on some predetermined storage medium, such as hard disk drive, in which case, the destination specification is omitted and (8-12) would be rewritten as

```
REWRITE(INFO);
```
(8-13)

If there is an existing file with the name INT.DATA already stored on the floppy disk which is on drive #9, then the REWRITE will cause all of the information in it to be erased. A sequential file can be considered to have a pointer that points to the place where data is to be written or read. The REWRITE statement erases the existing file and moves the pointer to the start of the file.

Every time that a file is established, a variable called a *buffer variable* is also set up. This represents the current "element" of the file. When data is to be written onto the file, it is first put into the buffer and then written into the file sequentially. After each item of data is written, the pointer is advanced to the next file location. The buffer variable name is the same as the name of the file in the program except that it has an up arrow added to it. Hence, the buffer name in program (8-1Ø) is

```
INFO↑
```
(8-14)

When we want to write information onto the file, we write

```
INFO↑:=C; PUT(INFO);
```
(8-15)

The first statment assigns the value of C to the buffer, and the second puts the value stored in INFO↑ onto the disk (or onto whatever storage is used). It is convenient to write both of these statements on the same line as shown in (8-1Ø).

Since the two statements of (8-15) are very often used together, a single PASCAL statement is provided to simplify the program. It is

```
WRITE(INFO,J);
```
(8-16)

In Sec. 8-4 we shall relate this to the WRITE statement that we have already discussed.

Now consider program (8-1Ø). Ten INTEGER values are read and stored in INFO. The file is actually stored under the name INT.DATA which is on device number 9. (Remember that this notation is not standard.)

Consider the statement

```
CLOSE(INFO,LOCK);                                    (8-17)
```

Whereas the REWRITE statement is said to "open" the file, the CLOSE statement "closes" it. When the CLOSE statement is executed, an *end of file mark* is put on the file. There is a PASCAL function called EOF. This is FALSE until the end of file mark is reached. The EOF can be used to terminate reading from a file in much the same way as the EOLN is used when reading of a line is terminated, see Sec. 6-5.

The LOCK is a command that insures that the file is saved. Note that the CLOSE statement is not standard, and that in some cases, the LOCK will not be needed. With some compilers, it is not necessary to write a statement that closes the file, since this is done automatically.

Now let us consider a program that reads the data written by program (8-1Ø).

```
PROGRAM INTDATFILREAD(INPUT,OUTPUT,INTFILE);
VAR INTFILE:FILE OF INTEGER;
    I,J:INTEGER;
BEGIN
  RESET(INTFILE,'#9:INT.DATA');                      (8-18)
  WHILE NOT EOF(INTFILE)DO
    BEGIN
      J:=INTFILE↑; GET(INTFILE);
      WRITE(J:3)
    END;
  WRITELN;
  CLOSE(INTFILE,LOCK)
END.
```

Note that the program FILE name here and the one in (8-1Ø) *need not be the same*. In this case, the program name of the file is INTFILE. In order to read a file, we must open it. We *cannot* use the REWRITE here, since that erases the file. Instead, the command

```
RESET(File name, source);                            (8-19)
```

is used. Note that the source name *must* be that of the file stored on the magnetic medium. Again, as in the case of REWRITE, with some computers the source is omitted. The RESET opens the file and moves the pointer to its beginning.

The name of the buffer is now INTFILE↑. In order to read the data from the file, we use

```
J:=INTFILE↑; GET(INTFILE);                    (8-2Ø)
```

Note that the GET command replaces the PUT command because now the data is being read instead of being written.

The instruction of (8-2Ø) can be replaced by the single PASCAL statement

```
READ(INTFILE,J);                              (8-21)
```

The READ and WRITE instructions of (8-21) and (8-16) are more convenient to use than the pairs of statements of (8-2Ø) and (8-15). Unfortunately, with *some* PASCAL compilers, the READ and WRITE statements can only be used with CHAR files. Your computer manual should be checked to ascertain which forms are available.

We wrote program (8-18) assuming that we did not know how much data was in the file. The EOF function was used. Now the WHILE-DO loop will cycle until EOF(INTFILE) becomes TRUE. However, note the NOT statement. Actually, the WHILE-DO loop will cycle until NOT EOF(INTFILE) becomes FALSE.

We have considered the reading and writing of a single item of data. However, more than one item can be entered or read. For instance, we can have

```
READ(NAME,A,B,C);                             (8-22a)
```

That is, a list of variables can be placed after the file name. Statement (8-22a) is equivalent to

```
READ(NAME,A);
READ(NAME,B);                                 (8-22b)
READ(NAME,C);
```

In a similar way, we can have a list of variables in a WRITE statement.

```
WRITE(NAME,A,B,C);                            (8-23)
```

If a sequential file contains 1ØØ items and we are only interested in the 78th one, we must read through all the intervening 77 variables. This can be done by assigning them to a dummy variable (i.e. one that is not used for any other purpose). For instance, we could have

```
FOR I:=1 TO 77 DO READ(NAME,DUMMY);           (8-24)
READ(NAME,B);
```

Now, B will be assigned the value of the 78th item in the NAME file.

8-3. STRINGS AND FILES

Let us now consider the reading and writing of strings on files. Actually, we shall discuss the use of PACKED ARRAYS in conjunction with files. The basic ideas of the last section apply here. Let us illustrate this with an example.

```
PROGRAM ARRFILWRITE(INPUT,OUTPUT,SAVE);
(*ILLUSTRATION OF WRITING A PACKED ARRAY TO A FILE*)
TYPE STRINGS=PACKED ARRAY[1 . . 10] OF CHAR;
VAR NAMES:ARRAY[1 . . 5] OF STRINGS;
    I,J:INTEGER;
    CH:CHAR
    SAVE:FILE OF CHAR;
BEGIN (*INITIALIZE ARRAY*)
  FOR I:=1 TO 5 DO
    BEGIN
      FOR J:=1 TO 10 DO NAMES[I,J] :=' ';                    (8-25)
    END;
  FOR I:=1 TO 5 DO (*WRITE DATA INTO ARRAY*)
    BEGIN
      J:=0;
      REPEAT
        J:=J+1;
        READ(CH);
        NAMES[I,J] :=CH;
      UNTIL EOLN;
      READLN
    END;
  (*FILE WRITING BEGINS HERE*)
  REWRITE(SAVE'#9:INFO,DATA'); (*OPEN FILE*)
  FOR I:=1 TO 5 DO WRITE(SAVE,NAMES[I] );
  CLOSE(SAVE,LOCK) (*CLOSE FILE*)
END.
```

The file is declared as discussed in the previous section. Note that much of the program enters data into the ARRAY, NAMES. Actually, each element of NAMES is a PACKED ARRAY representing a string. The actual FILE writing is performed in the second, third and fourth lines from the end. The REWRITE statement opens the file. The WRITE statement is used to put information into the array as was discussed in the last section. Note that even though the FILE is designated as a FILE of CHAR, we can use a single instruction to write an entire string contained in a PACKED ARRAY to the FILE. In this case.

```
        WRITE(SAVE,NAMES[I] );                                    (8-26)
```

writes the entire PACKED ARRAY, NAMES[I] to the file. The CLOSE statement is the same as that discussed in the last section.

Now let us consider a program that can be used to read the file generated by program (8-25).

```
PROGRAM ARRFILREAD(INPUT,OUTPUT,SAVE);
(*ILLUSTRATION OF READING OF CHARACTER DATA
        FROM A FILE*)
TYPE STRINGS=PACKED ARRAY[1 . . 1Ø] OF CHAR;
VAR NAMES:ARRAY[1 . . 5Ø] OF STRINGS;
    I,J,K:INTEGER;
    CH:CHAR;
    SAVE:FILE OF CHAR;
BEGIN
  RESET(SAVE,'#9:INFO.DATA');                                  (8-27)
  I:=Ø;
  K:=Ø;
  WHILE NOT EOF(SAVE) DO
    BEGIN
      I:=I+1;
      K:=K+1;
      FOR J:=1 TO 1Ø DO
        BEGIN
          READ(SAVE,CH);
          NAMES[I,J]:=CH;
        END;
    END;
  (*WRITE DATA TO SCREEN OR PRINTER*)
  FOR I:=1 TO K DO
    BEGIN
      FOR J:=1 TO 1Ø DO WRITE(NAMES[I,J] );
      WRITELN
    END;
END.
```

We have assumed that the number of items in the ARRAY is not known but that there are less than 5∅ strings, each of which is composed of 1∅ characters. Thus, we have used the EOF to terminate reading. Not all PASCAL compilers will allow us to read into a PACKED ARRAY merely by specifying its name in a single READ statement. That is, the converse of the writing operation of program (8-25) may not be possible. In such cases, the file must be read, one character at a time. Each character is then individually assigned to the array as is illustrated in program (8-27). In this program the resulting array is printed after the file is read. In an actual program, the data in the array might be manipulated. We have just simply output the data for illustrative purposes. The use of STRING, see Sec. 6-3, may resolve these problems. The discussion of the next section also can simplify these manipulations.

8-4. TEXT FILES

PASCAL allows the use of files that are specified as TEXT. Such files can be arranged into groups of lines of arbitrary length which is often convenient for word processing applications. An illustration of a program that organizes a TEXT file into a group of lines is

```
PROGRAM TEXTFILWRITE(INPUT,OUTPUT,SAVE);
(*ILLUSTRATION OF WRITING LINES TO TEXT FILES*)
VAR CH:CHAR;
    SAVE:TEXT;
BEGIN
   REWRITE(SAVE,'#9:INF.TEXT'); (*OPEN FILE*)
   REPEAT (*START OF OUTER LOOP*)
      READ(CH);
      WHILE((NOT EOLN)AND(CH<>'#'))DO (*START OF INNER
                                                LOOP*)
         BEGIN
            WRITE(SAVE,CH);                              (8-28)
            READ(CH)
         END; (*END OF INNER LOOP*)
      WRITELN(SAVE);
   UNTIL CH='#'; (*END OF OUTER LOOP*)
   CLOSE(SAVE,LOCK) (*CLOSE FILE*)
END.
```

SAVE is specified as TEXT, which designates it as a TEXT file. The FILE is opened using the REWRITE statement.

Now, when the statement WRITE(SAVE,CH) is executed, characters are read into the file. When the return is entered from the terminal, EOLN becomes TRUE. Now the inner loop terminates and the statement WRITELN(SAVE) is executed, which causes an end of line mark to be written to the file. The inner loop cycles again. Data for a new line is then written. When a # is entered, the procedure is terminated. The line lengths are aribitrary and need not be equal.

Now let us consider a program that reads the file.

```
PROGRAM TXTFILREAD(INPUT,OUTPUT,SAVE);
(*ILLUSTRATION OF READING LINES FROM TEXT FILES*)
VAR CH:CHAR;
    SAVE:TEXT;
BEGIN
   RESET(SAVE,'#9:INF.TEXT');                          (8-29)
   WHILE NOT EOF(SAVE)DO (*START OF OUTER LOOP*)
      BEGIN
         WHILE NOT EOLN(SAVE)DO (*START OF INNER LOOP*)
            BEGIN
               READ(SAVE,CH);
               WRITE(CH)
            END; (*END OF INNER LOOP*)
         READLN(SAVE);
         WRITELN
      END; (*END OF OUTER LOOP)
   CLOSE(SAVE,LOCK)
END.
```

In the inner loop, we read the file, one character at a time, until the end of the line mark is reached. Note that EOLN becomes TRUE when a return is entered. EOLN(SAVE) refers to an end of line symbol from file SAVE. Note that EOLN with no file specified is equivalent to EOLN (from input device). When EOLN(SAVE) becomes TRUE, the inner loop terminates. Now the statement READLN(SAVE) advances the pointer to the next "line" of the file SAVE which can now be read. Thus, the file will be read line by line until the end of file mark is reached and EOF(SAVE) becomes TRUE. In this simple program we read a file and then print it. Of course, after the file is read, more complex operations could be performed.

We can use TEXT files with arrays. For instance if, in program (8-25) we had designated file SAVE as TEXT, then we could replace the third line from the end with

```
FOR I:=1 TO 5 DO WRITELN(SAVE,NAMES[I] );
```

and this program could then be read by program (8-29).

8-5. INPUT AND OUTPUT—EXTERNAL FILES

We have considered that files are stored on magnetic media. Actually, in PASCAL, this need not be the case. When we output to a printer or to a screen, or we input from cards or a terminal, then PASCAL considers that we are writing to or reading from a file. The file used for output of data is called OUTPUT. In general, its meaning will vary. For instance, if you are operating in the batch processing mode, then the OUTPUT file will refer to the line printer, while if you are working with a terminal, the OUTPUT file will refer to the screen. If we want to output the values of A, B and C to the printer, we could use either the statement

```
WRITE(OUTPUT,A,B,C);                                    (8-30a)
```

or

```
WRITELN(OUTPUT,A,B,C);                                  (8-30b)
```

In all of the programs that we have used thus far, the word OUTPUT was not included with the WRITE or WRITELN statement. It is not necessary to do so. When the WRITE statement is used, the file is assumed to be OUTPUT, unless another one is specified. OUTPUT is said to be the *default* file for WRITE or WRITELN.

In a similar way, when the READ statement is used, a file called INPUT is assumed. That is, the ordinary READ statement that we used in previous chapters could have been written using the INPUT file name, for instance,

```
READ(INPUT,A,B,C);                                      (8-31a)
```

or

```
READLN(INPUT,A,B,C);                                    (8-31b)
```

Again, it is not necessary to indicate the word INPUT, since it is the default for the READ and READLN operations.

External Files

When we use a file to read from a keyboard, or to output to a terminal, or to read from or write on files stored on magnetic media that have existed before or will exist after the program is run, then such files are called *external files.* Note that, in program (8-25), if we did not LOCK the file then, after the program was run, the file would be lost. This is an example of an *internal* file. Files are usually external, but internal files are used to conserve memory when a great deal of data is to be stored temporarily during execution.

All external files must be declared in the program heading. This is why we include (INPUT,OUTPUT) in most of the program heads. For instance, in program (8-25), the file SAVE is also listed in the program heading. Note that not all PASCAL compilers require the inclusion of INPUT and OUTPUT files or any other files' names in the program heading.

Interactive Files

An *interactive file* is one which interacts with the person using the program. For instance, if you are using a terminal, then the INPUT and OUTPUT files are interactive. An interactive file can be declared in the program. This can be useful if you want to change the mode of input and/or output. For instance, suppose that you are working with a terminal but you want to direct the program's output to the line printer. Statements such as the following could be used.

```
VAR P:INTERACTIVE;
  :
  :
BEGIN                                    (8-32)
RESET(P,'PRINTER');
  :
  :
WRITELN(P,A.B.C);
```

Here we have declared P to be an interactive file and, in the RESET statement, declared it to be output to the printer. Now when the WRITELN statement is executed, the results will be directed to the printer insead of to the screen. The RESET statement, and not RE-

WRITE, should be used to open interactive files. Such files need not be closed. Note that the form of the interactive file operation may vary from computer to computer. Your computer manual should be checked to ascertain the proper form.

EXERCISES

1. What is meant by a user-defined data type?
2. Modify the program of Exericse 6-11 using user-defined statement types to make the program more self-documenting.
3. Repeat Exercise 3 for the program of Exercise 6-13.
4. Write a program that stores a list of 1ØØ REAL numbers. Then write another program that reads the file, multiplies all numbers by 2, and writes the results back to the original file. Check your program by running it on your computer.
5. Repeat Exercise 4 but now write the results to a new file.
6. Repeat Exercise 4 but now use INTEGER numbers.
7. Modify the program of Exercise 4 but now use the EOF function.
8. Write a program that inputs a list of names, and then stores them in a CHAR file. Now write another program that reads the file, alphabetizes the list of names, and then writes the results back to the original file. Check your program by running it on your computer.
9. Repeat Exercise 8 but now write a program that inputs the names from two separate lists and writes the alphabetized combined list as a new single file.
1Ø. Repeat Exercise 8 but now use TEXT files.
11. Repeat Exercise 9 but now use TEXT files.
12. What is meant by an internal file?
13. Why is it not necessary to use the name of the OUTPUT file in conjunction with the WRITE statement?
14. Discuss the use of interactive files.

Chapter Nine

Sets

Set theory is a branch of mathematics, many of whose operations are implemented in PASCAL. These operations can be of great use in the comparison, selection, and elimination of quantities in programs. In this chapter we shall discuss the PASCAL set operations. However, before proceeding, we shall first present a discussion of some of the basic ideas of set theory.

9-1. SOME ELEMENTARY IDEAS OF SET THEORY

In mathematics, a collection of objects is a *set*. For instance, we can have the set of integers or the set of prime numbers. We can also have collections of other things such as the set of people with brown eyes. The elements of a set are called the *members* of the set. In PASCAL, when we deal with sets, all of the members must be of the same TYPE.

Let us consider some simple sets. Although the mathematical notation for sets is braces, { } , we shall use square brackets, [ ], since this is the PASCAL symbolism. For instance, the set of all the capital letters is

[A,B,C,D,E,F,G,H,I,J,K,L,M,N,O,P,Q,R,S,T,U,V,W,X,Y,Z] (9-1)

The set of all the vowels is

[A,E,I,O,U] (9-2)

The set of all the odd numbers between Ø and 15 is

[1,3,5,7,9,11,13,15] (9-3)

If *all* of the members of one set are also members of another set, then the first set is *included* in the second. For instance, consider the set of all numbers between Ø and 5.

$$A = [Ø,1,2,3,4,5] \quad (9\text{-}4)$$

and the set of odd numbers between Ø and 5

$$B = [1,3,5] \quad (9\text{-}5)$$

The second set is included in the first one. The PASCAL notation would be

$$A >= B \quad (9\text{-}6)$$

This is read "A contains B." Similarly, we can state

$$B <= A \quad (9\text{-}7)$$

"B is contained by A." The mathematical notations for these are

$$A \supseteq B \quad (9\text{-}8)$$

and

$$B \subseteq A \quad (9\text{-}9)$$

The *union* of two sets is that set which contains all of the elements of both sets. For instance, the union of sets D and E given by

$$D = [Ø,1,3,5] \quad (9\text{-}1Øa)$$

$$E = [2,3,5,7] \quad (9\text{-}1Øb)$$

is

$$D+E = [Ø,1,2,3,5,7] \quad (9\text{-}11)$$

The PASCAL symbol for union is +, while the mathematical symbol is $\cup$.

The *intersection* of two sets is the set containing their common elements. The PASCAL symbol for intersection is the asterisk, *. The mathematical symbol for intersection is $\cap$. The intersection of sets D and E of (9-1Øa) and (9-1Øb) is

$$D*E = [3,5] \quad (9\text{-}12)$$

The converse of union is *relative complement*. For instance, the relative complement of D with respect to E are all those members of D which are not in E. For D and E as given by (9-1Ø), the relative complement of D with respect to E is

$$D-E = [Ø,1] \quad (9\text{-}13)$$

Note that the PASCAL symbol for relative complement is the minus sign, −.

The *empty* set is a set which has no elements. In PASCAL it is written as

[ ] (9-14)

The final set operation is *inclusion*. In PASCAL, the word IN is used, whereas the mathematical symbol is ∈. For instance, see (9-1∅a), 3 is included in D. Mathematically, we would write 3 ∈ D. In PASCAL

3 IN D

would be TRUE. That is, in PASCAL, the inclusion operation is a BOOLEAN one.

9-2. PASCAL SET MANIPULATIONS

Let us now illustrate set manipulation in PASCAL. All of the operation that were discussed in the last section are valid. In addition, the assignment operations can be used. Other operations, such as reading and writing, cannot be used with sets. Let us consider the following illustrative program

```
PROGRAM SAMPLESETUSE(INPUT,OUTPUT);
(*ILLUSTRATION OF BASIC SET OPERATIONS*)
TYPE DAY=SET OF(SUN,MON,TUES,WED,THURS,FRI,SAT);
     DIGIT=∅ . . 9;
VAR DAYS,WEEKEND,WORKTIME,WORKDAYS:DAY;
     INDEX,COUNTER:SET OF DIGIT;
     K:INTEGER;
     CH:CHAR;
 BEGIN
   WEEKEND:=[SUN,SAT] ; (*SET ASSIGNMENT*)
   WORKDAYS:=[MON,TUES,WED,FRI] ;
   DAYS:=WORKDAYS;
   IF DAYS=WORKDAYS THEN (*BOOLEAN EQUALITY*)
      WRITELN(' SETS EQUAL')
         ELSE WRITELN(' SETS UNEQUAL');
   WORKTIME:=[SUN,MON,THRUS,SAT] ;
   DAYS:=WORKDAYS*WORKTIME; (*INTERSECTION*)
```

```
IF DAYS=[MON] THEN WRITELN(' INTERSECTION');      (9-15)
DAYS:=WORKDAYS-WORKTIME; (*RELATIVE COMPLE-
                              MENT*)
IF DAYS=[TUES,WED,FRI] THEN WRITELN(' DIFFERENCE');
IF WEEKEND<=WORKTIME THEN WRITELN(' WORKED
                         ENTIRE WEEKEND');
IF WORKTIME>=WEEKEND THEN WRITELN('WORKED
                         ENTIRE WEEKEND');
DAYS:=WORKDAYS+WORKTIME; (*UNION*)
IF DAYS=[SUN,MON,TUES,WED,THURS,FRI,SAT] THEN
   WRITELN(' ENTIRE SET');
READLN(K);
INDEX:=[1,2,3,4,5] ;
IF K IN INDEX THEN WRITELN(' 1 TO 5');
IF K IN[15,16,17] THEN WRITELN(' 15 TO 17'); (*UNDE-
                  CLARED SET CONSTANT*)
READ(CH);
IF CH IN['A','E','I','O','U'] THEN WRITELN(' VOWEL')
   ELSE IF CH IN['A','E','I','O','U'] + ['Y'] THEN
      WRITELN(' LETTER Y') (*UNION OF UNDECLARED
                         SET CONSTANTS*)
END.
```

We start by declaring a user-defined TYPE DAY as a SET of [SUN, MON,TUES,WED,THURS,FRI,SAT] . In addition, DIGIT is declared as a subset of the INTEGERS. Then, DAYS, WEEKEND, WORKTIME, and WORKDAYS are sets of TYPE DAY. Note that this does *not* mean that each one contains all of the variables SUN, MON, TUES, WED, THURS, FRI, SAT but, rather, that these are the *only* variables that can be contained in these sets. Here, SUN, MON, TUES, WED, THURS, FRI, and SAT are called the *basic types* of the sets. In PASCAL, each set operation must be carried out with sets of the same basic type. We have also declared DIGIT to be a subgroup of TYPE INTEGER, and INDEX is declared to be a SET of TYPE DIGIT.

The first procedure illustrated in program (9-15) is SET assignment. The SET WEEKEND consists of [SUN,SAT] . Similarly, WORKDAYS is a SET consisting of [MON,TUES,WED,FRI] . Then the SET, DAYS is assigned the values of WORKDAYS. Now DAYS consists of [MON, TUES,WED,FRI] .

BOOLEAN comparisons are illustrated next. The equality operation is illustrated first. Since the SETS, DAYS and WORKDAYS, are equal, the words SETS EQUAL will be printed when the program is run. Next, the intersection and relative complement operations are illustrated. Both BOOLEAN expressions are TRUE, causing INTERSECTION and DIFFERENCE to be printed when the program is run. Next we have the BOOLEAN comparison, WEEKEND is contained in WORKTIME, and the expression WORKED ENTIRE WEEKEND will be printed. Similarly, since WORKTIME contains WEEKEND, the same statement will be printed. In other words, when the program is executed, WORKED ENTIRE WEEKEND will be printed twice. Although we have not illustrated it, the BOOLEAN inequality, < >, can also be used with SET operations.

Comparisons can be made between variables and set elements if they are of the same TYPE. For instance, the integer K is read. If it is in the SET INDEX, then 1 TO 5 will be printed.

If we use a set as a constant, then it does *not* have to be declared. We have defined a set [15,16,17] and used it to determine if the integer K is 15, 16, or 17. That is, we determine if it is in the set [15,16,17]. We have done the same thing with the vowels in the set ['A','E','I','O','U']. We can also work with the union and intersection of sets which are constants as well as with those that are variables. For instance, we performed

['A','E','I','O','U'] + ['Y'] = ['A','I','O','U','Y'] (9-16)

on the undeclared set constants. The operations of intersection and relative complement can also be used with SET constants.

Remember that the use of sets can simplify PASCAL programs which do not specifically manipulate sets. The number of elements that can be contained in a set is limited. A typical figure is 256. Your computer manual should be checked to determine the exact value.

EXERCISES

1. What is meant by a set?
2. Must all members of a SET be of the same TYPE in PASCAL?
3. What is meant by set union?
4. What is meant by set intersection?

5. What does it mean if one set is included in another one?
6. What is meant by relative complement?
7. Write a PASCAL program that compares two sets and determines if one is included in the other. Check your program by running it on your computer.
8. Write a PASCAL program that determines if the first letter of an entered word is a consonant. Check your program by running it on your computer.

Chapter Ten

The RECORD and Variant

We shall now consider some very versatile PASCAL operations. With all of the structured forms that we have considered thus far, such as the ARRAY or SET, only a single TYPE of data could be used. For instance, all of the elements had to be all REAL or all INTEGER, etc. We shall now discuss forms that are not limited in this manner.

1Ø-1. THE RECORD

The PASCAL language provides a structured form that, in many applications, is more convenient to use than the ARRAY. For instance, suppose that we want to work with the following information: a student's last name, first initial, and his grades in three tests. We then want to compute his average and then determine a letter grade based on the average. We could not store all this information in an array, since both CHAR and REAL data are used. The RECORD provides a convenient means of working with this information. We shall start by considering a RECORD that stores a single "line" of information. Then we shall extend this to an array of RECORDs.

Let us illustrate the use of the RECORD with a simple program that enters a student's last name, first initial, and grades in three tests. It then computes his average and supplies a letter grade.

```
PROGRAM SAMPLERECORD(INPUT,OUTPUT);
(*ILLUSTRATION OF THE USE OF THE RECORD*)
TYPE CLASS=RECORD
              LASTNAME:PACKED ARRAY[1 . . 1Ø] OF CHAR;
```

```
                FIRSTINITIAL,GRADE:CHAR;
                TEST1,TEST2,TEST3,AVERAGE:REAL
                END;
VAR SCIENCE:CLASS;
    J:INTEGER;
    CH:CHAR;
BEGIN
(*ENTER DATA*)
  FOR J:=1 TO 10 DO
    BEGIN
      READ(CH);
      SCIENCE.LASTNAME[J]:=CH
    END;
  READLN(SCIENCE.FIRSTINITIAL,SCIENCE.TEST1,
          SCIENCE.TEST2,SCIENCE.TEST3);                    (10-1)
  (*COMPUTE AVERAGE*)
  SCIENCE.AVERAGE:=(SCIENCE.TEST1+SCIENCE.TEST2+
                        SCIENCE.TEST3)/3.0;
  (*COMPUTE GRADE*)
  IF SCIENCE.AVERAGE>=90 THEN SCIENCE.GRADE:='A'
    ELSE IF SCIENCE.AVERAGE>=80 THEN
            SCIENCE.GRADE:='B'
      ELSE IF SCIENCE.AVERAGE>=70 THEN
            SCIENCE.GRADE:='C'
        ELSE IF SCIENCE.AVERAGE>=60 THEN
            SCIENCE.GRADE:='D'
          ELSE SCIENCE.GRADE:='F';
  (*WRITE DATA*)
  FOR J:=1 TO 10 DO WRITE(SCIENCE.LASTNAME[J]);
  WRITELN(SCIENCE.FIRSTINITIAL,'.',SCIENCE.GRADE:3)
END.
```

We start by declaring CLASS to be of TYPE RECORD. Note that we have

```
TYPE CLASS=RECORD
           LASTNAME:PACKED ARRAY[1 .. 10] OF CHAR;
           FIRSTINITIAL,GRADE:CHAR;                     (10-2)
           TEST1,TEST2,TEST3,AVERAGE:REAL
           END;
```

This means that all RECORDS of TYPE CLASS contain 7 elements called *fields*. The first field is a packed array of 10 characters called

LASTNAME, the next two fields are CHAR variables called FIRSTINITIAL and GRADE. The next four fields are REAL variables called TEST1, TEST2, TEST3, and AVERAGE. Note the END statement. A syntax diagram for the RECORD specification is shown in Fig. 1Ø.1.

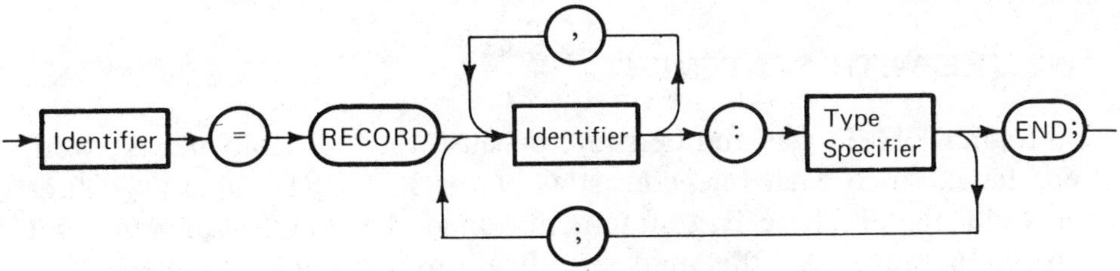

Figure 1Ø-1. Syntax diagram for the RECORD specification

Now consider the VAR statement. Here we declare SCIENCE to be of TYPE CLASS. Hence, SCIENCE is a RECORD with fields LASTNAME, FIRSTINITIAL, GRADE, TEST1, TEST2, TEST3, and AVERAGE.

The field variables are referred to by the RECORD NAME and their own name separated by a *period*. For instance, suppose that we want to assign 5Ø to TEST1. We would write

```
SCIENCE.TEST1:=5Ø
```
(1Ø-3)

Note that we could have more than one RECORD of TYPE CLASS. For instance, the VAR statement could be

```
VAR SCIENCE,BIOLOGY:CLASS;
```
(1Ø-4)

Now there would be two RECORDS, each with the same field specifier. This is why it is necessary to write both the RECORD name and the field specification. That is, BIOLOGY.TEST1 and SCIENCE.TEST1 would be different variables.

Now consider the program. The RECORD variables are treated as ordinary variables. For instance, SCIENCE.LASTNAME is a PACKED ARRAY. Bearing this in mind, the remainder of the program causes the necessary data to be entered and then the AVERAGE to be computed. Finally, a grade is assigned using the multiple IF-THEN-ELSE statement and the data is outputted.

Note that, in this program, the last name is assumed to consist of 1Ø letters or less and that, if less than 1Ø letters are printed, then blanks must be added. This problem could be resolved by using the EOLN function. It was not used here to avoid complicating the program.

We have used a PACKED ARRAY, but actually we could specify a PACKED RECORD in the TYPE statement. This would result in PACKing all the data of the RECORD. The advantages and limitations of such a procedure were discussed in Chapter 6.

1Ø-2. THE WITH STATEMENT

Program (1Ø-1) was cumbersome because the "variable names" were very large, since each one consisted of the RECORD name as well as the field name. There is a statement called the WITH statement that sets up a range. All the field specifications within that range act as though they were preceded by the RECORD name and a period. We shall illustrate this with the following program which is a modification of program (1Ø-1).

```
PROGRAM SAMPLERECORDWITH(INPUT,OUTPUT);
(*ILLUSTRATION OF THE USE OF THE WITH STATEMENT*)
TYPE CLASS=RECORD
           LASTNAME:PACKED ARRAY[1 . . 1Ø] OF CHAR;
           FIRSTINITIAL,GRADE:CHAR;
           TEST1,TEST2,TEST3,AVERAGE:REAL
           END;
VAR SCIENCE.CLASS;
    J:INTEGER;
    CH:CHAR;
BEGIN
WITH SCIENCE DO (*START OF WITH RANGE*)
  BEGIN
    FOR J:=1 TO 1Ø DO
      BEGIN                                                    (1Ø-5)
        READ(CH);
        LASTNAME[J]:=CH
      END;
    READLN(FIRSTINITIAL,TEST1,TEST2,TEST3);
    AVERAGE:=(TEST1+TEST2+TEST3)/3.Ø;
    IF AVERAGE>=9Ø THEN GRADE:='A'
      ELSE IF AVERAGE>=8Ø THEN GRADE:='B'
        ELSE IF AVERAGE>=7Ø THEN GRADE:='C'
          ELSE IF AVERAGE>=6Ø THEN GRADE:='D'
            ELSE GRADE:='F';
```

```
        FOR J:=1 TO 1Ø DO WRITE(LASTNAME[J] );
        WRITELN(FIRSTINITIAL,'.',GRADE:3)
     END; (*END OF WITH RANGE*)
  END.
```

The form of the WITH statement is

WITH Identifier DO Statement (1Ø-6)

The statement may be a compound PASCAL statement, as in (1Ø-5), where the compound statement starts with the BEGIN statement following the WITH statement and ends with the END statement associated with the comment (*END OF WITH RANGE*). The rule for matching the proper BEGIN and END statements is exactly the same as for other PASCAL statements. Now the program is more easily written than that of (1Ø-1) since the SCIENCE. does not have to precede all of the RECORD variable names.

Let us indicate a somewhat more versatile use of the WITH statement. Suppose that we are going to work with grades in the Biology class as well as in the Science class. We could modify program (1Ø-5) in the following way:

```
VAR SCIENCE,BIOLOGY:CLASS
  :
BEGIN                                                    (1Ø-7)
WITH SCIENCE DO
              }  Operations on SCIENCE RECORD
END;
WITH BIOLOGY DO
              }  Operations on BIOLOGY RECORD
END;
  :
```

Now we can perform a set of operations such as those in (1Ø-5) on the components of the SCIENCE RECORD. We can then perform a similar (or different) set of operations on the components of the BIOLOGY RECORD. For instance, we could modify the IF-THEN-ELSE statement to change the range of the letter grades.

1Ø-3. USE OF RECORD ARRAYS

We have thus far considered that a RECORD consists of a single set of data. For instance, in the examples of Secs. 1Ø-1 and 1Ø-2, computations using only a single student's grades could be performed. A RECORD can be a component of an array. Thus, we can conveniently work with many RECORDs. For instance, in the previous examples, we could process many students' grades. Let us illustrate this.

```
PROGRAM SAMPLERECORDARRAY(INPUT,OUTPUT);
(*ILLUSTRATION OF THE USE OF THE RECORD
          WITH ARRAYS*)
TYPE CLASS=RECORD
          LASTNAME:PACKED ARRAY[1 . . 1Ø] OF CHAR;
          FIRSTINITIAL,GRADE:CHAR;
          TEST1,TEST2,TEST3,AVERAGE:REAL
          END;
VAR SCIENCE:ARRAY[1 . . 1ØØ] OF CLASS;
    I,J,NUMBER:INTEGER;
    CH:CHAR;
BEGIN
(*ENTER DATA*)
  READLN(NUMBER);
  FOR I:=1 TO NUMBER DO (*OUTER LOOP*)
    BEGIN
      WITH SCIENCE[I] DO
        BEGIN (*START OF WITH RANGE*)
          FOR J:=1 TO 1Ø DO                              (1Ø-8)
            BEGIN
              READ(CH);
              LASTNAME[J]:=CH
            END;
          READLN(FIRSTINITIAL,TEST1,TEST2,TEST3);
          AVERAGE:=(TEST1+TEST2+TEST3)/3.Ø;
          IF AVERAGE>=9Ø THEN GRADE:='A'
            ELSE IF AVERAGE>=8Ø THEN GRADE:='B'
              ELSE IF AVERAGE>=7Ø THEN GRADE:='C'
                ELSE IF AVERAGE>=6Ø THEN GRADE:='D'
                  ELSE GRADE:='F'
        END; (*END OF WITH RANGE*)
    END; (*END OF OUTER LOOP*)
```

```
FOR I:=1 TO NUMBER DO
   BEGIN
      WITH SCIENCE[I] DO
         BEGIN (*START OF WITH RANGE*)
            FOR J:=1 TO 1Ø DO WRITE(LASTNAME[J] );
            WRITELN(FIRSTINITIAL,'.',AVERAGE:5:1,
                                             GRADE:3)
         END;
   END;
END.
```

Now we have declared SCIENCE to be an array, each of whose elements is of TYPE CLASS. Since there are 1ØØ elements in this array,

SCIENCE[1] ,SCIENCE[2] , . . . , SCIENCE[1ØØ]

are all RECORDS of TYPE CLASS.

In this program, NUMBER represents the total number of students, which must be less than 1ØØ. The outer loop cycles I between 1 and NUMBER. Now consider the statement

WITH SCIENCE[I] DO (1Ø-9)

For each value of I, this statement indicates a different RECORD, i.e., SCIENCE[1], SCIENCE[2], etc. Thus, the first time that the outer loop is cycled, all the RECORD variables act as though they were preceded by SCIENCE[1], (e.g. SCIENCE[1].FIRSTINITIAL). The second time through the loop, all the RECORD variables act as though they were preceded by SCIENCE[2]., etc. Thus, each cycle of the outer loop causes a student's data to be entered and his average and grade are computed. The program ends with another loop and WITH range that causes the required data to be printed. A WITH range that is nested *within* a loop should lie entirely within the loop. This is why program (1Ø-8) has two WITH statements.

1Ø-4. NESTED RECORDS

The field of a RECORD can itself be a RECORD. This allows the programmer to construct an almost endless variety of data storage. To illustrate the use of this, let us modify program (1Ø-8) so that an additional set of laboratory grades can be entered, their average computed, and a letter grade assigned for the laboratory. We shall write a separate RECORD for this and include it as a field in the RECORD of TYPE CLASS. The program is

```
PROGRAM SAMPLERECORD(INPUT,OUTPUT);
(*ILLUSTRATION OF THE USE OF NESTED RECORDS WITH
        ARRAYS*)
TYPE EXP=RECORD
        EXP1,EXP2,EXPAVE:REAL:
        EXPGRADE:CHAR
        END;
  CLASS=RECORD
        LASTNAME:PACKED ARRAY[1 . . 1Ø] OF CHAR;
        FIRSTINITIAL,GRADE:CHAR;
        TEST1,TEST2,TEST3,AVERAGE:REAL;
        LABORATORY:EXP
        END;
VAR SCIENCE:ARRAY[1 . . 1ØØ] OF CLASS;
    I.J,NUMBER:INTEGER;
    CH:CHAR;
BEGIN
  READLN(NUMBER); (*ENTER DATA*)
  FOR I:=1 TO NUMBER DO
    BEGIN (*START OUTER LOOP*)
      WITH SCIENCE[I] DO
        BEGIN (*START SCIENCE WITH RANGE*)
          WITH LABORATORY DO
            BEGIN (*START LABORATORY WITH RANGE*)
              FOR J:=1 TO 1Ø DO
                BEGIN
                  READ(CH);                        (1Ø-1Ø)
                  LASTNAME[J] :=CH
                END;
              READLN(FIRSTINITIAL,TEST1,TEST2,TEST3,
                              EXP1,EXP2);
              AVERAGE:=(TEST1+TEST2+TEST3)/3.Ø;
                              (*COMPUTE GRADES*)
              IF AVERAGE>=9Ø THEN GRADE:='A'
                ELSE IF AVERAGE>=8Ø THEN GRADE:='B'
                  ELSE IF AVERAGE>=7Ø THEN
                                 GRADE:='C'
```

```
                        ELSE IF AVERAGE>=6Ø THEN
                                          GRADE:='D'
                          ELSE GRADE:='F';
                 EXPAVE:=(EXP1+EXP2)/2.Ø;
                 IF EXPAVE>=9Ø THEN EXPGRADE:='A'
                   ELSE IF EXPAVE>=8Ø THEN
                                    EXPGRADE:='B'
                     ELSE IF EXPAVE>=7Ø THEN
                                      EXPGRADE:='C'
                       ELSE IF EXPAVE>=6Ø THEN
                                        EXPGRADE:='D'
                         ELSE EXPGRADE:='F'
               END; (*END OF LABORATORY WITH RANGE*)
           END; (*END SCIENCE WITH RANGE*)
       END; (*END OUTER LOOP*)
     FOR I:=1 TO NUMBER DO (*PRINT RESULTS*)
       BEGIN
         WITH SCIENCE[I],LABORATORY DO (*START SCIENCE,
                                  LABORATORY WITH RANGE*)
           BEGIN
             FOR J:=1 TO 1Ø DO WRITE(LASTNAME[J]);
             WRITELN(FIRSTINITIAL,'.',AVERAGE:5:1,
                 GRADE:3,EXPAVE:5:1,EXPGRADE:3)
           END; (*END SCIENCE,LABORATORY WITH RANGE*)
       END;
   END.
```

We declare EXP to be a TYPE of RECORD with REAL fields, EXP1, EXP2, and EXPAVE. In addition, the field EXPGRADE is of TYPE CHAR. Now, when the RECORD of TYPE CLASS is declared, one of its fields is of TYPE RECORD EXP. This is equivalent to CLASS's having an additional four fields which are those of EXP. In this simple program, we could have simply extended CLASS. However, program (1Ø-1Ø) illustrates the use of nested RECORDS. There are times when we might want to use the same nested RECORD with two different "main" RECORDs, in which case, such a procedure would be convenient. The nested RECORD must be declared before any RECORD that uses it.

Now let us consider the program. We declare SCIENCE to be a RECORD of TYPE CLASS in the VAR statement. Note that LABOR-

ATORY has already been declared a RECORD of TYPE EXP in the TYPE declaration of the RECORD CLASS. Now, in the execution portion of the program (which follows the first BEGIN) we use two nested WITH statements.

```
WITH SCIENCE[I] DO
   BEGIN
      WITH LABORATORY DO
         BEGIN
```

Now, within the range of both WITH statements, we have effectively prefixed each field specifier with SCIENCE[I]. and, where it is needed, with

```
LABORATORY.
```
(1Ø-11)

For instance, within the WITH range FIRSTINTIAL is effectively

```
SCIENCE[I].FIRSTINITIAL
```
(1Ø-12)

while EXP1 is effectively

```
SCIENCE[I].LABORATORY.EXP1
```
(1Ø-13)

Note that the second WITH statement need not immediately follow the first one. If, however, the two WITH statements follow each other, then they can be combined. For instance,

```
WITH SCIENCE[I] DO
   BEGIN
      WITH LABORATORY DO
```
(1Ø-14)

can be written as

```
WITH SCIENCE[I],LABORATORY DO
```
(1Ø-15)

Note that there is one less BEGIN here so that one less END is needed. (The BEGIN and associated END are only needed when a compound statement is used.) A syntax diagram for the WITH statement is given in Fig. 1Ø-2. The use of the WITH statement which uses two RECORD names is illustrated towards the end of program (1Ø-1Ø) where the data is printed.

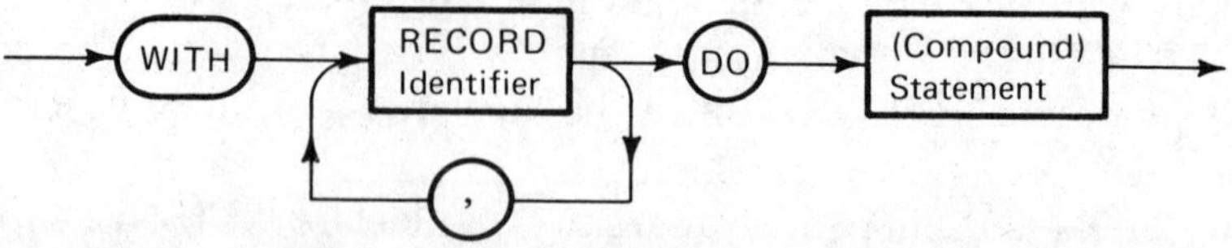

Figure 1Ø-2. Syntax diagram for the WITH statement

The fields of a nested RECORD can be specified without using the WITH statement. We have already illustrated this in (1∅-12) and (1∅-13). Once a RECORD name is used in a WITH statement, it should not be explicitly used within the range of the WITH statement. For instance, the prefix LABORATORY. should not be used within the ranges of the WITH statements of program (1∅-1∅).

The degree of nesting that can be used will vary with the compiler. Your computer manual should be checked to determine the allowed degree.

1∅-5. RECORD VARIANTS

There are times when we want to vary the form of a RECORD during the execution of the program. This is called a RECORD with a *variant*. For instance, suppose that, in the grading program (1∅-8), we now want to enter two different grades for two different classes, PHYSICS and BIOLOGY. The grades in the PHYSICS tests will be numerical, while letter grades A, B, C, D, and E are given in the BIOLOGY tests. Note that the letter E is used rather than F. This is done to simplify a grading algorithm so that the program is not obscured with details that do not relate to variants. Before we start the program, let us consider the declaration of a RECORD with a variant.

```
TYPE DIR=(PHYSICS,BIOLOGY);
GRD='A'..'E';
CLASS=RECORD
        LASTNAME=PACKED ARRAY[1..2∅] OF CHAR;
        FIRSTINITIAL,GRADE:CHAR;
        AVERAGE:REAL;                                  (1∅-16)
        CASE TAG:DIR OF
                PHYSICS:(TEST1,TEST2,TEST3:REAL);
                BIOLOGY:(TESTA,TESTB,TESTC:GRD);
        END;
```

Note the CASE statement. This specifies the variant part of the RECORD declaration. This is similar to the CASE statement discussed in Chapter 4 but there are some differences. In essence, these are two different RECORDs, one with the PHYSICS variant and one with the BIOLOGY variant. Note that both variants have some common field specifiers, i.e. LASTNAME, FIRSTINITIAL, GRADE, and AVERAGE. In the PHYSICS variant, the fields TEST1, TEST2, and TEST3 are REAL, while in the BIOLOGY variant, TESTA, TESTB, and TESTC are designated as CHAR. When the program is run, the variable TAG will determine which fields are used. The variant part of the RECORD declaration *must follow the fixed part*.

The CASE statement is actually a combination of two statements.

```
TAG:DIR
CASE DIR OF
```
(1∅-17)

In contrast to the ordinary CASE specifier, the CASE selector is a TYPE, not a variable. Also, there is no END statement required here. This is because the *variant* CASE must always come at the *end* of the RECORD specifications, and so that PASCAL language is written so that only one END statement suffices.

The variable TAG is called a *tag field* specifier. Note that it can be any valid PASCAL name. TAG does not have to be used. A syntax diagram for the RECORD specification is shown in Fig. 1∅-3.

Now let us consider the program.

```
PROGRAM SAMPLERECORDVARIANT(INPUT,OUTPUT);
(*ILLUSTRATION OF THE USE OF RECORD VARIANTS*)
TYPE DIR=(PHYSICS,BIOLOGY);
     GRD='A' . . 'E';
     CLASS=RECORD
              LASTNAME:PACKED ARRAY[1 . . 2∅]OF CHAR;
              FIRSTINITIAL,GRADE:CHAR;
              AVERAGE:REAL;
              CASE TAG:DIR OF
                 PHYSICS:(TEST1,TEST2,TEST3:REAL);
                 BIOLOGY(TESTA,TESTB,TESTC:GRD)
              END;
VAR SCIENCE:ARRAY[1 . . 1∅∅] OF CLASS;
    I,J,K,NUMBER:INTEGER;
    CH:CHAR;
    TAG:DIR;
BEGIN
   READLN(CH,NUMBER); (*ENTER DATA*)
   IF CH='P' THEN TAG:=PHYSICS
      ELSE TAG:=BIOLOGY;
   FOR I:=1 TO NUMBER DO (*START OF OUTER LOOP*)
      BEGIN
```

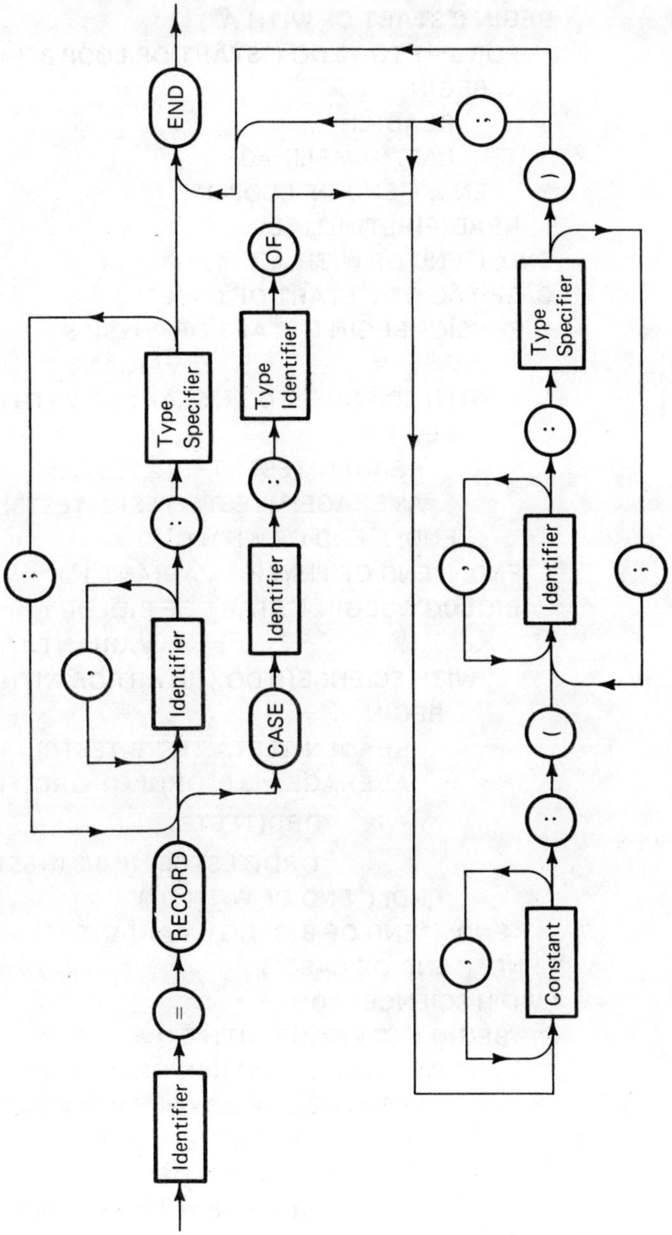

Figure 1Ø-3. Syntax diagram for the RECORD specification with variant

```
WITH SCIENCE[I] DO
   BEGIN (*START OF WITH A*)
      FOR J:=1 TO 1Ø DO (*START OF LOOP B*)
         BEGIN
            READ(CH);
            LASTNAME[J] :=CH
         END; (*END OF LOOP B*)
      READ(FIRSTINITIAL)
   END; (*END OF WITH A*)
   CASE TAG OF (*START OF CASE*)
      PHYSICS:BEGIN (*START OF PHYSICS
                                 VARIANT 1*)
         WITH SCIENCE[I] DO (*START OF WITH C*)
            BEGIN
               READLN(TEST1,TEST2,TEST3);
               AVERAGE:=(TEST1+TEST2+TEST3)/3.Ø
            END; (*END OF WITH C*)
      END; (*END OF PHYSICS VARIANT 1*)
      BIOLOGY:BEGIN (*START OF BIOLOGY
                                 VARIANT 1*)
         WITH SCIENCE[I] DO (*START OF WITH D*)
            BEGIN                                        (1Ø-18)
               READLN(TESTA,TESTB,TESTC);
               AVERAGE:=(3.Ø*ORD('E')–ORD(TESTA)–
                       ORD(TESTB)
                       ORD(TESTC))*1Ø.Ø/3.Ø+55.Ø;
            END; (*END OF WITH D*)
      END; (*END OF BIOLOGY VARIANT 1*)
   END; (*END OF CASE*)
   WITH SCIENCE[I] DO
      BEGIN (*START OF WITH E*)
         IF AVERAGE>=9Ø THEN GRADE:='A'
            ELSE IF AVERAGE>=8Ø THEN GRADE:='B'
               ELSE IF AVERAGE>=7Ø THEN
                          GRADE:='C'
                  ELSE IF AVERAGE>=6Ø THEN
                             GRADE:='D'
                     ELSE GRADE:='F'
      END; (*END OF WITH E*)
```

```
      END; (*END OF OUTER LOOP*)
      FOR I:=1 TO NUMBER DO (*PRINT RESULTS*)
        BEGIN
          WITH SCIENCE[I] DO
            BEGIN
              FOR J:=1 TO 1Ø DO WRITE(LASTNAME[J] );
              WRITELN(FIRSTINITIAL,'.',AVERAGE:5:1,
                                        GRADE:3)
            END;
        END;
    END.
```

We have discussed the declaration part. Note that TAG is declared to be of TYPE DIR. We shall use TAG both as a tag field specifier and as an ordinary CASE specifier.

When the program is run, the first data that is input is a letter which indicates whether the PHYSICS or the BIOLOGY RECORD and calculations are to be used, and the number of students. Then, using the IF-THEN-ELSE statement, TAG is assigned the value of either PHYSICS or BIOLOGY. Next, data for the last name and first initial are read. This data uses the fixed part of the RECORD.

Consider the CASE statement. It divides the program into two branches. In each of these, a WITH statement again specifies the RECORD. The variable TAG now not only selects the branch of the CASE statement within the body of the program, but it is also used to select the desired branch of the variant. Note that TAG acts in two different ways here. It chooses the branch of the CASE statement, and with the CASE and WITH statements, also causes the selection of the desired variant of the RECORD. Note that only one CASE statement is required and it includes a WITH statement. Remember that the field specifier and the CASE selectors were chosen to have the same identifier.

In general, if the range of a WITH statement starts within a loop, then the range cannot extend beyond the loop. Thus, an additional WITH statement is used for printing. Since none of the variant specifiers are used here, no variant selection is necessary.

EXERCISES

1. What is meant by a RECORD?
2. Use a RECORD in a program to store the batting averages of baseball players. Store first and last names, times at bat, hits, and batting averages. Check your program by running it on your computer.
3. Modify the program of Exercise 2 to use WITH statements.
4. Write a program using RECORDs that accepts the following information: first and last names, middle initial, address, and birthdate, and prints out the name and birthday or the name and address for a mailing label.
5. Repeat Exercise 3 but now accept the entire team's records. Have the program print out all the data. Check the program by running it on your computer.
6. Repeat Exercise 5 but now allow the person running the program to enter a single name and have that individual player's data printed out.
7. Repeat Exercise 4 but now enter data for 1ØØ people, print out a list of names and birthdays and a list suitable for use as mailing labels.
8. Repeat Exercise 7 but now have the data for one person printed when the name is entered.
9. Write a program using RECORD variants that stores a first and last name, address, birthday, social security number, income, and tax paid. One branch of the program provides a mailing list based on birthday, while the other branch of the program provides tax information. Check the program by running it on your computer.
10. Write a program for a company, using RECORD variants, that enters the names and addresses of customers, and either the total amount of purchases or the names of five items purchased from the company by each customer. One branch of the program is to be used for billing purposes; the other branch is for market research. Check the program by running it on your computer.

Chapter Eleven

Dynamic Data Structures

The variables that we have discussed thus far are called *static* variables. They are declared in the VAR statement and exist as long as the program or subprogram in which they are declared is running. That is, memory locations are reserved for these variables during compilation and, as long as the (sub)program is running, these memory locations are exlcusively used to store these variables. Remember that array sizes are also declared so that every static variable has a memory location allocated to it and these do not change during the running of the (sub)program. Although this situation is satisfactory for many programs, there are times when another situation would be desirable. For instance, suppose that several long lists of data are to be input. If we stored this in several arrays, we would have to size each array so that it could store the maximum amount of data that *might* be entered. The memory of the computer might not be large enough for this. However, if not every list were of maximum size, then there might be enough memory to store all the data. For instance, suppose that there were four lists, each of which *might* contain 1Ø,ØØØ elements. If we used arrays, then each one would be sized [1 . . 1Ø,ØØØ], and there might not be enough available memory. On the other hand, during a typical run of the program, the number of items of data entered might be 2ØØØ, 4ØØØ, 5ØØ, 1Ø,ØØØ or perhaps, 1Ø,ØØØ, 2ØØØ, 3ØØØ, 1ØØØ, and there might be enough storage space for either of these.

If we do not allocate storage space before the execution of the program, but only allocate it as it is needed, then this is termed *dynamic data storage*. PASCAL provides for this and we shall discuss it in this chapter.

If we are to use dynamic data storage, then there must be memory locations reserved for the program. In PASCAL, these memory locations are called the *heap*.

11-1. DYNAMIC DATA STORAGE

A *dynamic variable* can be created during the execution of a PASCAL program. What this means is that, during execution, memory locations can be assigned for data storage. (Note that a variable can be stored in more than one memory location.) These memory locations are in the heap. Remember that the heap is just a set of memory locations reserved for this program. Once a dynamic variable is created, it remains until it is destroyed. The act of destroying a dynamic variable means that the locations in the heap are disassigned. Now these memory locations are free to be used by another variable.

Static variables are referred to by an identifier, but dynamic variables are not. Instead, they are referred to by their location in the heap. To do this, another variable called the *pointer variable* is established. This indicates (or points to) the memory locations that store the dynamic variable. The programmer does not have to keep track of the actual memory locations. Indeed, he will probably not even know them. Note that there are two data values that correspond to each dynamic variable; one is the value of the variable itself and the other is its pointer. (When data is stored statically, the identifier acts as a pointer.) This is diagrammatically illustrated in Fig. 11-1. In Fig. 11-1a, a pointer points at memory locations a. The pointer can be used to access all the data stored there. The data stored in memory locations a can be a RECORD so that several different items can be stored there. In Fig. 11-1b, we have three pointers and many memory locations. Now pointer 1 or pointer 2 can be used to access the data stored in memory locations a, while pointer 3 can be used to access the data stored in memory locations c. Remember that a pointer is just (stored) data that tells us where the data for the dynamic variable is stored. In the situation shown, we cannot access the data in the other memory locations since we do not know where they are. However, the data is usually stored in a RECORD, one or more of whose fields stores the data for the pointers to other memory locations. For instance, after the data in memory locations a is accessed, we might obtain the pointer to memory locations b. Now these memory locations can be accessed. We have assumed that the data is stored in the form of a RECORD. This need

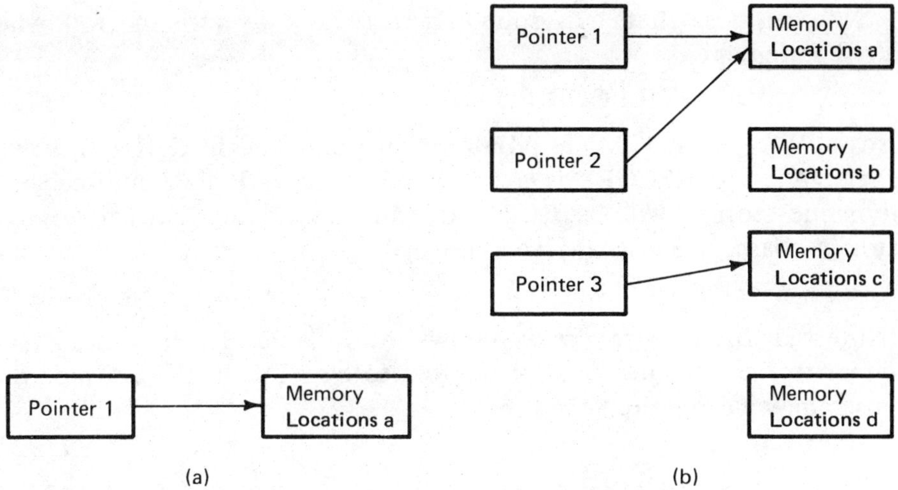

Figure 11-1. An illustration of pointers. (a) A simple case; (b) A case with several pointers

not be the case but, because of the varied nature of the information to be returned, it is desirable to work with the data in a RECORD. For instance, consider the following declaration.

```
TYPE POINT=↑DYNDAT;
     DYNDAT=RECORD
               A:REAL;                    (11-1)
               NUMB:INTEGER;
               LOOK:POINT
               END;
```

Now, DYNDAT is a TYPE specification for a RECORD which will be used for dynamic data storage. The actual data in this case is of TYPE REAL which is stored in field A, and of TYPE INTEGER which is stored in the field NUMB. The field LOOK stores pointer data. The pointer for RECORDs of TYPE DYNDAT is written as an up arrow followed by the RECORD TYPE. Hence, we have

```
↑DYNDAT                                   (11-2)
```

for the TYPE of POINT. Note that when we specify POINT as being of TYPE ↑DYNDAT, then specifying a RECORD TYPE of the same identifier (without the up arrow) indicates that RECORDs of this type will be used for dynamic data storage. The compiler then "knows" how much memory to allocate.

Now suppose that, corresponding to (11-1) we have the following VAR statement

```
VAR PTR,LOOK:POINT;                                  (11-3)
```

Now, PTR and LOOK are pointers that point to RECORDs of TYPE DYNDAT. The RECORD is *not* declared in the VAR statement because dynamic storage will be used, and thus we do not have to reserve storage space. In PASCAL, we write

```
PTR↑                                                 (11-4)
```

(Note that the up arrow now follows the variable.) In this case, PTR↑ refers to the dynamic variable pointed to by PTR. In the body of the program, we can write

```
B:=6;                                                (11-5)
PTR↑.NUMB:=B;                                        (11-6)
```

This refers to the memory locations pointed at by PTR, the actual field designated by NUMB. Thus, statements (11-5) and (11-6) will store an integer 6 in field NUMB of the memory locations pointed at by PTR. We could also write PTR↑.NUMB:=6;.

The programmer has no way of determining the pointer values since the memory allocation scheme is not known. However, PASCAL has a built in procedure that automatically assigns the next available memory location on the heap to a pointer. The procedure is called NEW. For instance,

```
NEW(PTR);                                            (11-7)
```

will assign the next available memory location to PTR. That is, this information will be assigned to PTR. To illustrate these ideas, let us write a program that inputs a list of numbers, stores them dynamically, and then outputs the list.

```
PROGRAM SIMPLEDYNAMICDATA(INPUT,OUTPUT);
(*ILLUSTRATION OF ELEMENTARY DYNAMIC DATA*)
TYPE POINT=↑DYNDAT;
     DYNDAT=RECORD
               NUMB:INTEGER;
               A:REAL;
               LOOK:POINT
               END;
```

```
VAR PTR,SEEK:POINT;
    X:REAL;
    I:INTEGER;
BEGIN
  PTR:=NIL;
  SEEK:=PTR;
  READLN(X,I);
  WHILE X>-1E6 DO                                              (11-8)
    BEGIN
      NEW(PTR); (*GET NEW POINTER VALUE*)
      PTR↑.LOOK:=SEEK; (*STORE OLD POINTER VALUE*)
      PTR↑.A:=X; (*STORE DATA*)
      PTR↑.NUMB:=I;
      SEEK:=PTR; (*UPDATE SEEK*)
      READLN(X,I)
    END;
  (*OUTPUT LIST IN REVERSE ORDER*)
  WHILE PTR<>NIL DO (*ONLY (IN)EQUALITY
                                        COMPARISONS*)
    BEGIN
      WRITELN(PTR↑.A,PTR↑.NUMB:5);
      PTR:=PTR↑.LOOK
    END;
END.
```

Let us consider the operation of this program. The declaration is as discussed. Now consider the execution part of the program. We start by assigning the pointer PTR to NIL. NIL is a PASCAL value that can be assigned to a pointer which *does not* point to a memory location. It can be used to indicate that all the data has been read. We now set a second pointer SEEK:=PTR. This is an illustration of assignment with pointers.

Data for the first values of X and I is then read. Now we enter the loop and execute

```
NEW(PTR);                                                      (11-9)
```

which assigns a value to PTR from the heap. Note that the TYPE statement defines the form of the RECORD to which pointers of TYPE POINT will point. In this case, space is reserved for an INTEGER, a REAL, and a variable of TYPE POINT. The statements

```
PTR↑.LOOK:=SEEK;        (11-1∅a)
PTR↑.A:=X;              (11-1∅b)
PTR↑.NUMB:=I;           (11-1∅c)
```

are in the form of a RECORD assignment. However, in this case, the RECORD is not assigned a memory location at compilation. Its memory location is assigned during execution when PTR is given a value.

Note that the value stored in the field LOOK is the value of SEEK which is the "old" value of PTR. Now SEEK is updated to the present value of PTR. The loop then keeps cycling until a value of X<=−1E6 is entered.

Now the stored data is read and printed. Note that the only PTR value that is known is the last one used. This points to the last RECORD. Hence, that data can be obtained and, in this case, the desired items are output. In addition, the RECORD stores the "preceding" pointer value. This value is assigned to PTR; it is said to *update* PTR. Now the next to last RECORD can be obtained and the desired data printed. A new value of PTR is obtained. This procedure continues until the value obtained for PTR becomes NIL.

Because of the way that data is stored in the computer, we cannot assume that PTR is incremented in any uniform way. Thus, in order to use the dynamic data storage, we must have some method of storing the pointer values in the RECORD as was illustrated. For instance, we *cannot* print out the data in the same order in which it was entered by setting PTR:=NIL and then writing NEW(PTR); to obtain the first pointer value. The procedure NEW will seek out unused locations in the heap and meaningless data will be printed.

Quasidynamic Data Storage

We can store pointer values in an array for use at a later time. This tends to nullify the basic advantages of dynamic data storage. We could use an array to store the data for all the pointers as static variables. However, we would now have to allocate a fixed amount of storage for the pointers. The procedure might have some meaning if each RECORD contained many dynamic variables. Then space might be allocated to one array to statically store the pointer data alone, while a great many variables would be stored dynamically. This could be called *quasi-*

dynamic storage. Let us illustrate this with a program that is similar to (11-8). Now we can access the data in any order.

```
PROGRAM QUASIDYNAMICDATA(INPUT,OUTPUT);
(*ILLUSTRATION OF QUASIDYNAMIC DATA*)
TYPE POINT=↑DYNDAT;
      DYNDAT=RECORD
                 NUMB:INTEGER;
                 A:REAL
                 END;
VAR PTR:POINT;
     X:REAL;
     I,J,K:INTEGER;
     Q:ARRAY[1..5Ø] OF POINT;                    (11-11)
BEGIN
  J:=Ø;
  PTR:=NIL;
  READLN(X,I);
  WHILE X>-1E6 DO
    BEGIN
      J:=J+1;
      NEW(PTR); (*GET NEW POINTER VALUE*)
      Q[J]:=PTR;
      PTR↑.A:=X;
      PTR↑.NUMB:=I;
      READLN(X,I)
    END;
  FOR K:=1 TO J DO WRITELN(Q[K]↑.A,Q[K]↑.NUMB:5)
END.
```

This is similar to program (11-9) but now the RECORD does not contain a pointer field, and all references to SEEK are deleted. We set up a Q ARRAY of TYPE POINT. The pointer values are then stored in Q. These values can then be used to print the data. Note that this procedure is limited in comparison with true dynamic storage in that the size of the Q array must be specified. However, the procedure may be useful for some applications.

The procedure NEW allocates enough memory to hold the entire RECORD if the RECORD has a variant(s). Then data will be allocated for all the fields in each variant(s). The procedure NEW can be modified to choose the desired variant. For instance, suppose that there are two variants, PHYSICS and BIOLOGY, in the RECORD. Then we could write

```
NEW(PTR,PHYSICS);                                (11-12)
```

Now the PHYSICS variant would be used and memory space would be conserved. This use of NEW does not select the tag field in the operation of the program and this must be done as discussed in Sec. 1Ø.5. Note that this procedure should be avoided except by experienced programmers. Different compilcrs may treat statements of the form of (11-12) in different way and errors may result without any warning.

11-2. REUSING DYNAMIC STORAGE

There are times when data is stored in the heap and processed. We then have no further use for it. In such cases, it would be desirable to be able to free the memory locations so that they could store other data. This would conserve storage space. PASCAL provides several procedures for this. However, not all versions of PASCAL provide all the procedures that we shall discuss. Your computer manual should be checked to determine the ones that are available.

The first procedure that we shall discuss makes use of the procedures MARK and RELEASE. The forms of the instructions are

```
MARK(HEAP);                                      (11-13)
```

and

```
RELEASE(HEAP);                                   (11-14)
```

where HEAP *must* be declared as a pointer.

When the MARK procedure is used, it places a "mark on the heap." When the subsequent RELEASE command is given, all of the data locations that were assigned subsequent to the execution of MARK are freed and the computer can reassign these locations to other variables. The old data should then be considered to be lost. These instructions can only be used to release data from the "end" of the heap. We cannot take an existing heap and remove memory from its "middle" using MARK and RELEASE.

As an example of the use of MARK and RELEASE we shall rewrite program (11-8). Now three sets of data will be entered. After the first set is entered, the heap will be marked and then a second set of data will be entered. Then all the data will be printed (in reverse order). After this, the heap will be released and a third set of data will be entered. The released memory locations can now be used (and others added if needed) for storage of the third set of data. Finally, the third and first sets of data will be printed out (in reverse order). Remember that the second set of data is now lost.

```
PROGRAM DYNAMICDATAREALLOCATION(INPUT,OUTPUT);
(*ILLUSTRATION OF DYNAMIC DATA REALLOCATION*)
TYPE POINT=↑DYNDAT;
     DYNDAT=RECORD
              NUMB:INTEGER;
              A:REAL;
              LOOK:POINT
              END;
VAR PTR,SEEK,HEAP,REF:POINT;
    X:REAL;
    I:INTEGER;
BEGIN
  PTR:=NIL;
  SEEK:=PTR;
  READLN(X,I);
  WHILE X>-1E6 DO
    BEGIN
      NEW(PTR); (*GET NEW POINTER VALUE*)
      PTR↑.LOOK:=SEEK; (*STORE OLD POINTER VALUE*)
      PTR↑.A:=X;
      PTR↑.NUMB:=I;
      SEEK:=PTR; (*UPDATE SEEK)
      READLN(X,I)
    END;
  REF:=PTR; (*SAVE THIS POINTER VALUE*)
  MARK(HEAP); (*HEAP MARKED HERE*)
  READLN(X,I); (*REPEAT DATA ENTERING*)
  WHILE X>-1E6 DO
    BEGIN
      NEW(PTR);                                        (11-15)
      PTR↑.LOOK:=SEEK;
      PTR↑.A:=X;
      PTR↑.NUMB:=I;
      SEEK:=PTR;
      READLN(X,I)
    END;
```

```
        (*OUTPUT LIST IN REVERSE ORDER*)
        WHILE PTR<>NIL DO
           BEGIN
              WRITELN(PTR↑.A,PTR↑.NUMB:5);
              PTR:=PTR↑.LOOK
           END;
        RELEASE (HEAP); (*HEAP RELEASED BACK TO MARK*)
        SEEK:=REF; (*SEEK SET TO POINTER VALUE BEFORE
                                       MARK*)
        READLN(X,I); (*REPEAT READ IN PROCEDURE*)
        WHILE X>-1E6 DO
           BEGIN
              NEW(PTR);
              PTR↑.LOOK:=SEEK;
              PTR↑.A:=X;
              PTR↑.NUMB:=I;
              SEEK:=PTR;
              READLN(X,I)
           END;
        WHILE PTR<>NIL DO (*WRITE ORIGINAL DATA AND
                                       REWRITTEN DATA*)
           BEGIN
              WRITELN(PTR↑.A,PTR↑.NUMB:5);
              PTR:=PTR↑.LOOK
           END;
     END.
```

The first part of the program is essentially the same as that of (11-8). We define HEAP to be of TYPE PTR. A new pointer variable REF is defined. It is set equal to the last used value of PTR before MARK is executed. Now additional data is entered and the results are printed. The operation of the program up to this point is essentially the same as that of (11-8). Now the RELEASE is executed and the second set of data should be considered to be lost. New data is entered and the results are printed. Note that we do not know if the old data was overwritten. If we had saved the pointer values for the second set of data, we might still find it stored. However, this is *very bad* programming practice. The data could be written over. Do not RELEASE data unless you *never* want to use it again.

The use of MARK and RELEASE does not allow us to reuse locations in the "middle of the heap." That is, we can only RELEASE locations at the end of the heap. On some versions of PASCAL there is a procedure called DISPOSE that does allow the reusing of locations other than those at the end of the heap. An example of its use is

```
DISPOSE(PTR);                                        (11-16)
```

Now the memory locations pointed at by PTR are RELEASEd and can be reused.

```
   :
DISPOSE(PTR);
   :                                                 (11-17)
HOLD↑.A:=X;
HOLD↑.NUMB:=I;
```

HOLD must be a pointer. The new variables might be stored in the old locations. The computer keeps track of all the available locations on the heap and assigns them as needed. Then the disposed locations can be used again. Once a location has been "disposed" its data should be considered to be lost.

11-3. DYNAMIC DATA STRUCTURES

We can use dynamic data procedures to create various *data structures*. We shall discuss some of these ideas here. The actual ideas behind the optimum choice of dynamic data structures is beyond the scope of this book.

Let us start by considering that we have a list of variables and that we want to insert data in the "middle" of the list. For instance, suppose that we input 15 numbers and, at a later time, we input 3 other numbers. When the list is printed we want these 3 numbers to appear embedded within the original 15. This does *not* involve changing the location of the data on the heap. Actually, the data may be anywhere on the heap. The locations of the data items are not determined until the program is executed. To achieve the desired results we must use the pointers in the proper order. The following program illustrates this. It is a modification of program (11-8) in that a list of variables is entered. Next a number N is entered. After this, a new list of variables is entered. When the results are printed, the new list will be embedded in the old one, N terms from the end. The program is

```
PROGRAM DYNAMICDATAMANIPULATION(INPUT,OUTPUT);
(*ILLUSTRATION OF DYNAMIC DATA MANIPULATION*)
TYPE POINT=↑DYNDAT;
      DYNDAT=RECORD
                NUMB:INTEGER;
                A:REAL;
                LOOK:POINT
                END;
 VAR PTR,SEEK,HOLD,REF,MAX:POINT;
      X:REAL;
      I,J,N:INTEGER;
 BEGIN
   PTR:=NIL;
   SEEK:=PTR;
   READLN(X,I);
   WHILE X>-1E6 DO
      BEGIN
        NEW(PTR); (*GET NEW POINTER VALUE*)
        PTR↑.LOOK:=SEEK; (*STORE OLD POINTER VALUE*)
        PTR↑.A:=X;
        PTR↑.NUMB:=I;
        SEEK:=PTR; (*UPDATE SEEK*)
        READLN(X,I)
      END;
   READLN(N); (*INSERT DATA N BACK IN LIST*)
   MAX:=PTR;
   HOLD:=PTR;
   FOR J:=1 TO N-1 DO HOLD:=HOLD↑.LOOK; (*GET POINTER
                                   N-1 ITEMS BACK IN LIST*)
   REF:=HOLD↑.LOOK; (*GET POINTER N ITEMS BACK IN
                                              LIST*)
   SEEK:=REF;
   READLN(X,I); (*ENTER DATA FOR INSERTION IN LIST*)
```

```
WHILE X>-1E6 DO
   BEGIN
      NEW(PTR);
      PTR↑.LOOK:=SEEK;
      PTR↑.A:=X;
      PTR↑.NUMB:=I;
      SEEK:=PTR;
      READLN(X,I)                                    (11-18)
   END;
HOLD↑.LOOK:=PTR;
(*OUTPUT LIST IN REVERSE ORDER*)
PTR:=MAX;
WHILE PTR<>NIL DO
   BEGIN
      WRITELN(PTR↑.A,PTR↑.NUMB:5);
      PTR:=PTR↑.LOOK
   END;
END.
```

The program enters a list of data just as in (11-8). After this is done, a number N is entered. Each RECORD contains the pointer location for the preceding term in the list. Thus the RECORDs must be modified to account for this. We then read back through the last N−1 terms to obtain the value of the pointer stored in the N−1 RECORD. Its value will be temporarily stored in HOLD. Now we get the preceding pointer value and store it in REF. When the new list of data is entered, the pointer for the last entered item will be put into HOLD↑.LOOK (which is "in" the original list). Hence, after N terms of the original list are processed, the pointer will point to the last RECORD of the new list. Next SEEK is set equal to REF. When the RECORD for the new list is set up, the program is such that REF will be the pointer value stored in the first RECORD. Hence, after the new list is read backwards, the pointer will point back to the RECORD for the N+1 term from the end of the old list.

Now when the data is printed, the last N terms of the original list will be printed. Now the pointer data stored in the N RECORD from the end will point to the end of the new list and not to the N+1 RECORD of the old list. Now the new list will be printed in reverse order. After these RECORDs are read, the pointer will point back to the original list, N+1 terms from the end, and the remaining terms will be printed in reverse order.

Note that we can have data in various parts of the heap. However, it can be organized by proper manipulation of the pointer. For instance, suppose that we have three unrelated lists as diagrammatically shown in Fig. 11-2 and also suppose that the pointer address stored in the first RECORD of each list is NIL, while the last RECORDs stored in list a and list b are pointed at by pointer 1 and pointer 2, respectively. (Pointer 1 and pointer 2 represent address data.)

Now suppose that we change the data stored in the first RECORD of lists b and c so that the pointer information in the first RECORD of list c is that for pointer 2 and, similarly, the pointer information in the first RECORD of list b is that of pointer 1. Now suppose we "read" backwards through list c. After its first RECORD is read, the pointer points to the last RECORD of list b. Now it will be read, etc. The three lists are said to be *linked* and the entire structure is called a *linked list*.

We can set up lists that loop back on themselves. These are called *rings*. For instance, in Fig. 11-2, if the pointer value stored in the first RECORD of list a becomes that of pointer 3, then a ring will be established. Such rings are often helpful when recursive procedures are used.

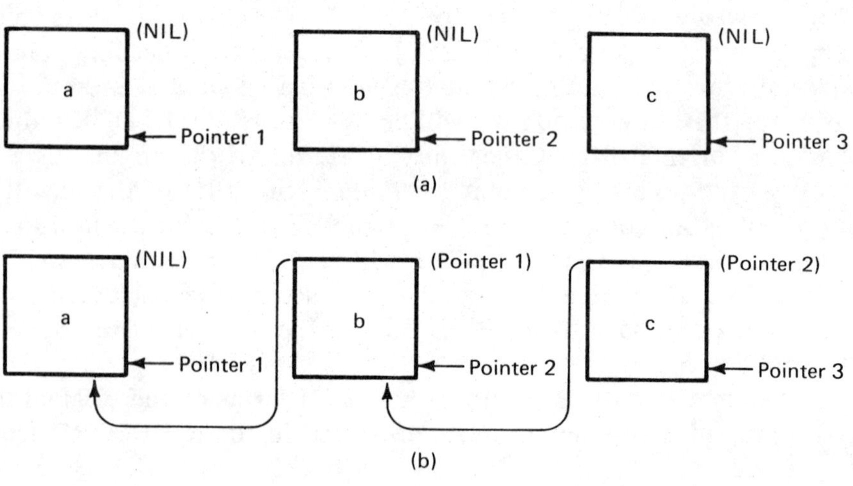

Figure 11-2. (a) Three unrelated lists; (b) a linked list obtained by storing appropriate pointer values

There are other structures that can be established. For instance, in Fig. 11-3, we illustrate a *tree* dynamic data structure. Now each list

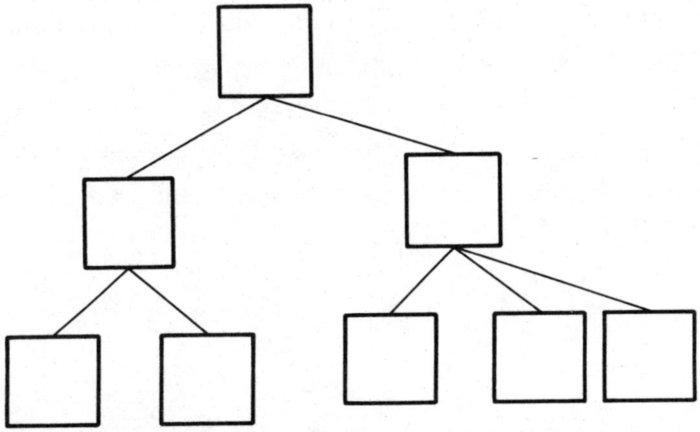

Figure 11-3. A tree dynamic data structure

may be linked with more than one other list. Of course, at any one time, the program will only follow one "branch" of the tree. We have considered RECORDs that store information concerning only one pointer. Actually, each RECORD can store the data for two or more pointers. The appropriate branch can be chosen by choosing the appropriate pointer data using an IF-THEN-ELSE or CASE operation. Relatively sophisticated programming techniques can be performed using such data structures.

EXERCISES

1. Contrast static and dynamic variables.
2. When might dynamic variables be used?
3. What is meant by a pointer?
4. What is the difference between a pointer and the memory location to which it points?
5. Write a program that will input a list of names and grades in 3 tests as a list of dynamic variables. Print out the list (in reverse order). Check the program by running it on your computer.

6. Modify the program of Exercise 5 so that each student's average in the three tests is also stored in the RECORDs and printed out.
7. Modify the program of Exercise 6 so that the last N items in the list are "removed" from the heap and then more data is entered.
8. Write a program that links three separately entered lists. Check the program by running it on your computer.
9. Modify the program of Exercise 8 so that a loop is obtained.
10. Write a program that sets up 8 lists in the tree structure of Fig. 11-3.

Appendix A

PASCAL Keywords

In this appendix, we list the PASCAL keywords. Examples of their use will be given as well as the section in which they are defined.

Keyword	*Example*	*Section Defined*
AND	IF C AND D THEN A:=Ø;	4-1
ARRAY	NAME:ARRAY[1 . . 5Ø] OF CHAR;	5-1
BEGIN	BEGIN	1-3
CASE	CASE NUMB OF	4-6
CONST	CONST PI=3.14159;	2-6
DIV	I DIV J;	2-2
DO	FOR I:=1 TO 1Ø DO	4-3
DOWNTO	FOR I:=1Ø DOWNTO 1 DO	4-3
ELSE	IF I=J THEN A:=B ELSE A:=Ø;	4-2
END	END.	1-3
FILE	SAVE:FILE OF CHAR;	8-2
FOR	FOR I:=1 TO 1Ø DO	4-3
FUNCTION	Y:=QBRT(X);	7-3
GOTO	GOTO 1ØØ;	7-3
IF	IF I=J THEN C:=Ø.2;	4-2
IN	IF A IN[1,2,3] THEN C:=Ø;	9-1
LABEL	LABEL 1ØØ;	4-8
MOD	X:=I MOD J;	2-2
NIL	POINT:=NIL;	11-1
OF	ARRAY[1 . . 5Ø] OF INTEGER;	5-1
OR	IF C OR D THEN I:=K;	4-1
PACKED	PACKED ARRAY[1 . . 1ØØ] OF CHAR;	6-4

PROCEDURE	PROCEDURE QBRT(VAR X:REAL;Y:REAL);	7-1
PROGRAM	PROGRAM ADD(INPUT,OUTPUT);	1-3
RECORD	RECORD NAME:STRINGS; NUMBER:INTEGER END;	1Ø-1
REPEAT	REPEAT	4-4
SET	VOWEL=SET OF CHAR;	9-2
THEN	IF A=B THEN C:=Ø	4-2
TO	FOR I:=1 TO N DO	4-3
TYPE	TYPE STRINGS=PACKED ARRAY [1 . . 5Ø] OF CHAR;	5-2
UNTIL	UNTIL A>B	4-4
VAR	VAR I,J,K:INTEGER;	1-3
WHILE	WHILE A>B DO	4-4
WITH	WITH NAME[I] DO	1Ø-2

Appendix B

PASCAL Library Functions

Here we list the PASCAL library subprograms. Although not all of these programs will be available at all installations, most of them should be. Where appropriate, we shall indicate the TYPE of the FUNCTION and the TYPE of the argument(s).

Definition	*Function*	*TYPE of Function*	*TYPE of Argument(s)*
|x| absolute value of x	ABS(X)	REAL	REAL
$\tan^{-1}(x)$	ATAN(X) or ARCTAN(X)	REAL (radians)	REAL
concatenation of strings	CONCAT(ST1,ST2)	STRING	STRING
cos(x)	COS(X)	REAL REAL	REAL INTEGER
end of file	EOF(X)	BOOLEAN	
end of line	EOLN(XO	BOOLEAN	
e^x	EXP(X)	REAL REAL	REAL INTEGER
insert S2 into S1, starting before the N1 character of S1	INSERT(S2,S1,N1)	STRING	STRING, STRING, INTEGER
length of string	LENGTH(S1)	INTEGER	STRING

ln(x)	LN(X)	REAL REAL	REAL INTEGER
log(x)	LOG(X)	REAL REAL	REAL INTEGER
true if x odd, false if x even	ODD(X)	BOOLEAN	INTEGER
ordinal value of x	ORD(X)	INTEGER	CHAR
print on next page	PAGE(FILE)		
predecessor of x	PRED(X)	INTEGER INTEGER	CHAR User-Defined TYPE
integer found by rounding x	ROUND(X)	INTEGER	REAL
sin(x)	SIN(X)	REAL REAL	REAL INTEGER
x^2	SQR(X)	REAL INTEGER	REAL INTEGER
$\sqrt{x}$	SQRT(X)	REAL	REAL
successor of x	SUCC(X)	INTEGER INTEGER	CHAR User-Defined TYPE
integer formed by truncation of x	TRUN(X)	INTEGER	REAL

Appendix C

PASCAL Structure TYPES

This is a list of the standard PASCAL TYPES and the sections in which they are defined.

Type	*Section*
INTEGER	2-2
BOOLEAN	4-1
REAL	2-1
CHAR	6-1
STRING (not standard on all compilers)	6-3
TEXT	8-4

Appendix D

PASCAL Operators

The PASCAL operators and the sections in which they are defined are listed here.

Arithmetic Operators

+	2-1
–	2-1
*	2-1
/	2-1
DIV	2-2
MOD	2-2

BOOLEAN Operators

AND	4-1
NOT	4-1
OR	4-1

Relational Operators

=	4-1
<>	4-1
>	4-1
>=	4-1
<	4-1
<=	4-1

Index

ABS, 33
Addition, 11
Adjusted, 48
Algorithm, 32, 76
Alphanumeric, 103
AND, 58
ARCTAN, 33
Argument, 32
Arithmetic, 23
ARRAY, 87
  assignment of, 97
  declaration of, 88
  element of, 88
  logical expression with, 97
  multidimensional, 94
  of RECORDs, 172
  PACKED, 110, 116

Basic type of set, 164
Batch processing, 2
BEGIN, 8
BOOLEAN, 55
Branch, 197
Bubble memory, 2
Buffer, 46
Buffer variable, 151
Bug, 19

Card reader, 2
Carriage control character, 50
CASE, 73
  user defined TYPE with, 148
CASE selector, 75
CHAR variable, operations with, 106
Character, 103
Character data, input of, 103
CHR, 107
CLOSE, 150, 152
Comment, 9
Compiler, 3
Compound statement, 12, 62
Computer, 1
  digital, 1
Conditional looping, 67
CONST, 35
Constant, 35
Contained by, 162
Contains, 162
Control, 55
COS, 33

Data, 42
Data FILE, 149
Data structure, dynamic, 193
Debug, 19
Debugging, 139
Default, 158
Destination, 150
Digital computer, 1
Disk, floppy, 2
  hard, 2
DISPOSE, 193
DIV, 25
Division, 14
DO, 65
DO loop, 65
Documentation, 79
DOWNTO, 66
Dynamic data, 183
Dynamic data structure, 193
Dynamic variable, 184

E, 13
Editor, 16
Element, 88
ELSE, 60
END, 8
EOF, 152
EOLN, 157
Equal, 56
Exponential notation, 13
EXTERN, 135
External FILE, 159

FALSE, 55
Field, 169
Field variable, 169
Field width, 45
  control of, 47

FILE, 149
  external, 159
  INPUT, 158
  INTERACTIVE, 159
  internal, 159
  OUTPUT, 158
  TEXT, 156
  with storage, 154
Final value, 67
Floppy disk, 2
Flow chart, 77
FOR, 65
Formatting, 47
FORWARD reference, 134
FUNCTION, 128
  library, 31
FUNCTION parameter, 136

Global variable, 124
GOTO, 80
GOTOless program, 80
Greater than, 56
Greater than or equal to, 56

Hard copy, 2
Hard disk, 2
Heading, PROCEDURE, 122
Heap, 184
Hierarchy, 28
Hierarchy diagram, 137

Identifier, 4
IF, 59
  nested, 64
IN, 163
Inclusion, 163
Index, 65
  user defined, 147

Index specifier, 89
Initial value, 67
INPUT FILE, 158
INTEGER, 24
INTERACTIVE FILE, 159
Internal FILE, 159
Intersection, 162

Justified, 48

Keyword, 7
Key punch, 17

LABEL, 80
Language, machine, 3
  programming, 3
Less than, 56
Less than or equal to, 56
Library FUNCTION, 31
Linked list, 196
Literal, 38
LN, 32
LOCK, 150
LOG, 32
Log in, 16
Logical operator, 58
Loop, nested, 72
Looping, conditional, 67
  unconditional, 65

Machine language, 3
Magnetic storage, 2
Main memory, 1
MARK, 190
Member, 161
Memory, 1
  bubble, 2
  word of, 116
Mixed mode, 30
MOD, 26
Module, 137
Multidimensional array, 94
Multiplier, 14

Negation, 28
Nested IF, 64
Nested loop, 72
Nested parentheses, 30
Nested RECORD, 173
Nested subprogram, 132
NEW, 186, 190
NIL, 187
NOT, 58
Not equal, 57
Null, 12
Number, ordinal, 107

Operator, logical, 58
  relational, 56
OR, 59
ORD, 107
Ordinal number, 107
OUTPUT FILE, 158
Overflow, 14

Packed ARRAY, 110, 116
Parameter, FUNCTION, 136
  PROCEDURE, 136
  value, 125
  variable, 123
Parentheses, 29
  nested, 30
PASCAL, 3
PASCAL character, 4
Passed, 125
Pointer, 184

PRED, 34, 107
PROCEDURE, 121
  with ARRAYs, 127
  heading of, 122
  parameters of, 136
Program, 1
Programming language, 3
Prompt, 16, 50
Printing of text, 49
Private variable, 123
Pseudolanguage, 76
Public variable, 124
PUT, 151

Quasidynamic data, 188

READ, 41, 153, 158
READLN, 41, 158
REAL, 9, 23
RECORD, 167
  ARRAY using, 172
  nested, 173
  variant, 177
Recursive use of subprograms, 130
Reference, FORWARD, 134
Relational operator, 56
RELEASE, 190
REPEAT, 68
Reserved word, 7
RESET, 152
Returns, 32
REWRITE, 150
Right adjusted, 48
Right justified, 48
Ring, 196
ROUND, 33

Self-documenting, 79
Sequential data FILE, 149
Set, 161
  basic type of, 164
  contained by, 162
  contains, 162
  included in, 162
  inclusion, 163
  intersection, 162
  number of, 161
  union, 165
Set constant, 165
SIN, 33
Specifier, index, 89
SQRT, 31
Statement, 12
  compound, 62
Static variable, 183
String, 103, 109
  with FILEs, 154
Structured programming, 55, 75, 137
Subprogram, 121
  nested, 132
  recursive use of, 130
Subrange, 147
Subscript, 87
Subtraction, 14
SUCC, 34, 107
Symbol +, 23
Symbol -, 23
Symbol *, 23
Symbol /, 23
Syntax diagram, 5

Tag field specifier, 178
TAN, 33
Terminal, 2
  video, 2
Text, printing of, 49
TEXT FILE, 156
THEN, 60

Timesharing, 15
TO, 65
Top down design, 137
Tree, 197
TRUE, 55
TRUNC, 34
Truncate, 34
TYPE, 92
  subrange of, 147
  user defined, 145

Unconditional jump, 80
Unconditional looping, 65
Underflow, 14
Union, 162
UNTIL, 68
User defined TYPE, 145
  with case, 149

Value parameter, 125
VAR, 9, 36
Variable, dynamic, 184
  field, 169
  global, 124
  pointer, 184
  private, 123
  public, 124
  static, 183
Variable parameter, 123
Variant of RECORD, 171
Video terminal, 2

WHILE, 70
WITH, 170
Word, 116
WRITE, 45, 151, 153, 158
WRITELN, 8, 45, 158